Master Your Investment in the Family Business
How to increase after-tax wealth

Larry Frostiak and Jenifer Bartman

WINNIPEG, MANITOBA, CANADA

Larry Frostiak and Jenifer Bartman

MASTER YOUR INVESTMENT IN THE FAMILY BUSINESS
How to increase after-tax wealth

Printed and bound in Canada

Library and Archives Canada Cataloguing in Publication

Frostiak, Larry H
        Master your investment in the family business : how to increase after-tax wealth / Larry Frostiak and Jenifer Bartman.

Includes index.
ISBN 978-1-897526-08-8

        1. Family-owned business enterprises—Canada—Management.
2. Family-owned business enterprises—Succession—Canada.
3. Family-owned business enterprises—Taxation—Canada.
I. Bartman, Jenifer, 1966- II. Title.

HD62.25.F76 2009   658'.045   C2009-906122-8

Publisher:
Knowledge Bureau, Inc.
187 St. Mary's Road, Winnipeg, Manitoba Canada R2H 1J2
204-953-4769 Email: reception@knowledgebureau.com

Publisher and Managing Editor: Evelyn Jacks
General Manager: Norine Harty
Editorial Assistance: Brenda Griffith
Cover and Page Design: Sharon Jones

Acknowledgements

Thank you to all of our great clients and businesses that we have met along the way who have inspired us to write this book.

It is our sincere hope that this book will help family businesses everywhere to reach higher levels of success and accomplishment.

We would also like to express our thanks to our families and business associates for their support and encouragement.

LARRY FROSTIAK AND JENIFER BARTMAN

Knowledge Bureau®

Presents
Financial Education for Decision Makers

The Master Your Personal Finances Books:

Master Your Taxes
How to maximize your after-tax returns

Master Your Retirement
How to fulfill your dreams with peace of mind

Master Your Money Management
How to manage the advisors who work for you

Master Your Real Wealth
How to live your life with financial security

Master Your Philanthropy
How to maximize your strategic giving

Master Your Investment in the Family Business
How to increase after-tax wealth

FREE UPDATING SERVICES

Keep up your Mastery! For the latest in tax and personal financial planning strategies subscribe to Breaking Tax and Investment News. Visit www.knowledgebureau.com/masteryourtaxes

Knowledge Bureau®

Contents

Introduction

Small- to medium-sized businesses make up a significant portion of Canada's business community and account for a large portion of the economic activity in this country. Most of us either know someone who runs a business or owns a business, or perhaps you are a business owner yourself. You may be an employee of a business, that may be owned and/or managed by an independent group of parties, or perhaps it is owned by an individual or family. Sometimes businesses start off as closely held family businesses that later become more widely held, perhaps by parties including the original owners, or perhaps by parties independent of the founder.

Consider the following:

Everyone has to start somewhere... and so most new businesses begin as small businesses. Some businesses stay small, some grow moderately, while others grow to become very large businesses, perhaps with operations spanning a number of countries. Some businesses operate for a period of time, experience moderate growth, and then fade into decline. Others, sadly, are wound up and no longer exist, often when the owner retires. Performance, profitability, and value can vary significantly from business to business, with some companies being sought after by customers, partners, and potential acquirers. Others go virtually unnoticed.

Why do some companies grow while others do not? Why do some businesses become the recognized name or "provider of choice" within their industry, while others fall to "commodity" status? Why do some companies remain strong throughout the years, perhaps even over generations, while others flounder when the original driving forces behind the business are no longer involved?

Is this a product of circumstance, luck, or something else? Most of us have heard stories of great business owners who seemingly had an opportunity dropped into their lap many years ago, and it was at that point that their future prospects changed for the better. Although this type of situation can and does occur (and often the greater the ultimate success of the enterprise, the greater the drama of the tale!), the reality is that an individual or group of individuals can indeed have a significant impact in building a business, particularly in terms of the perspective they bring and the lessons and example they pass to others.

More often, the ongoing success of a family business is the result of a vision to make a great product or provide an outstanding service, a defined strategy, process, and plan for its development, a sufficiently-sized target market and effective marketing plan, and astute business acumen that integrates effective fiscal management with the right amount of investment capital for growth.

The success of the family business, dynamics within the family unit, and ongoing financial planning that leads to an enduring legacy, perhaps an inter-generational transition, also has much to do with the work of professional advisors. Accountants, lawyers, insurance, and financial advisors, as well as those with specific expertise in terms of raising capital and leading business transactions, can all help business owners plan and structure income requirements now and in retirement for each family member. They can also help manage various risk factors and tax erosion all along the way to a successful transition of the business entity to the next generation of owners. The big win, for a family that masters their investment in the family business, is the realization of significant tax free gains when the company is sold.

This book, *Master Your Investment in the Family Business: How to increase after-tax wealth*, is designed to help you with just that. It will provide insight as to how those involved with a family business can effectively grow and maintain what is typically one of the most significant assets held by a family—whether it was borne out of economic necessity, or the driving vision and passion of its owners to meet a specific need or make a difference in the community.

More important, many families do not realize that the survival of their business may be at significant risk. Baby Boomer founders are now of retirement age and are faced with the reality of what the next steps for their business could be. *Yet, they typically do not start their succession planning early enough.*

Will the family business survive the transition to the next generation? How will the founders fund their retirement and receive a return on their investment? How will the next generation of business leaders cope with the multifaceted challenge of how to take a business forward into the future—into a world characterized by market volatility, rapid change, shrinking profit margins, increased regulatory requirements and public scrutiny, and the rising presence of environmental issues?

Do you know what you don't know? You must have a firm handle on tax planning opportunities, for example. From planning tax-efficient owner-manager compensation, to the delivery of perks and benefits to family members and other employees working in the business, to income splitting opportunities, maximization of the small business deduction, and the use of various business structures that could include everything from sole proprietorships to corporate operating companies, holding companies, and family trusts. You need to understand the impact in terms of timing the application of business losses on spending decisions and how "estate freezes" can help to position family members to utilize the lucrative capital gains deduction when a sudden opportunity to sell the family business arises.

There is much more to consider—but no one can be an expert at it all. That is why you need a team approach to Master Your Investment in the Family Business.

So, what's in it for you? If you need to know more in order to make important decisions for your family and your business, this book can help. In fact, reading this book may be one of the most important decisions you make today, because your investment in yourself and your family can be improved, now and in the future.

By learning new ways to build better professional relationships and sharpen your decision making skills, you will have greater opportunity to master a more powerful and secure investment in your family business, and ensure that sustainable wealth and a lasting legacy are built for the family.

THE FORMAT OF THIS BOOK

The principles for Mastering Your Investment in the Family Business are discussed in this book in a straight-forward fashion, with common features to empower your decision making skills. In each chapter, you will find:

- *A True to Life Scenario:* These feature fictitious families in real-life situations and are a backdrop for the principles discussed in the chapter.
- *The Issues:* What is important and why?
- *The Solutions:* What do you need to know and do to make the right financial decisions? How can you best integrate these solutions into your strategic plan to meet your goals?
- *The Mastery:* Tips and Traps to help you put your financial decision making into focus, simplify your efforts, and get better results.

We hope you will find this format useful in taking control and making better financial decisions, either on your own or together with your team of financial advisors.

LARRY FROSTIAK, JENIFER BARTMAN,
AND THE KNOWLEDGE BUREAU

CHAPTER 1

Entrepreneurial Spirit: Lifestyle vs. Market Driven Businesses

More than one way to raise the roof.

Michael and David, friends since elementary school, are both business owners in the housing industry.

David, an electrician, has been working on job sites since the age of 18. He launched his own electrical business after spending a number of years working for others, and is known for his good quality work, reliability, and friendly rapport with customers. Most of his work comes from word of mouth and he has a steady workload, which is especially busy during the summer months. David has not had to advertise for work; in fact, sometimes he has to turn down work, which he doesn't like to do. He simply does not have any time available. His wife handles the bookkeeping and coordinates the calls and daily work schedule, enabling David to focus solely on the technical requirements and his customers.

Michael, a finishing carpenter, acquired an interest in windows while he gained work experience in an upscale subdivision, and left his employment to purchase a small business from a founder who was near retirement and did not have a succession plan. Michael's high quality custom work was renowned for its unique designs. More importantly, production by his larger competitors typically took months longer than

Michael's. As the business grew, he got his two brothers involved, one as Sales Manager and the other as Production Manager, and additional staff members were hired. After a few years of growth, Michael and his brothers found a larger building and moved the business. Their collaboration was so successful that the brothers are now planning to open a second manufacturing facility. They are also receiving sales inquiries from other parts of the country and investigating distribution options to support sales in other geographic areas.

David is very happy for his friend, but often wonders why his company has not grown quite as well.

THE ISSUES

Michael and David are both family business owners, but there is a significant difference between their business operations. Although both are successful, highly regarded, and recognized for good quality work, their businesses are operating on two different levels.

David learned a skill or trade that could be readily sold in the market-place, *thereby creating a job for himself.* He pursues the amount of work necessary to meet his family's economic requirements.

Michael has taken a different approach to identifying opportunities. He is not averse to taking a risk to try something new. He has responded to needs in the marketplace, and as a result, the business has grown, in terms of sales, customers, and staff members. Michael has positioned his business to capitalize on an opportunity, one of the key characteristics of *an entrepreneur.*

An entrepreneur is defined by the Cambridge Dictionary as "someone who starts their own business, especially when this involves seeing a new opportunity." In recent years and particularly in the context of the recent global financial crisis that has left many unemployed, the notion of "entrepreneur" and "entrepreneurial" has been used excessively in context after context:

"I am looking for an entrepreneurial opportunity."
"I want to do something entrepreneurial."

"I want to work for an entrepreneurial company."

Many of these comments seem to suggest that the word entrepreneurial is a green light for all things unstructured and flexible, where anything and everything goes and represents an opportunity worth pursuing.

While "ideas" and "building" are of particular importance in entrepreneurship, the enterprise itself will only flourish when those passions are in fact delivered in the context of a well-thought-out, tax-efficient financial plan. Yet, it is for that very reason that so many businesses fail. Consider this:

- **Some family businesses exist to meet the economic needs of the family unit.** The founder generates business within his or her network, which ultimately represents the company's customer base, and does not have any significant initiative to grow beyond this point, so long as the family's economic needs are met. This type of business, illustrated by David, can be referred to as a *Lifestyle Family Business*.

- **Some family businesses are opportunity driven, in that the founder wishes to identify unmet needs or areas of potential within the marketplace and seek to position the business to meet and benefit from these needs.** This may involve developing new products and services, delivering products and services in a manner that exceeds what is currently available in the marketplace, or perhaps envisioning ways of doing things that do not currently exist. The founder in this scenario is motivated to grow the business beyond the current economic needs of the family, and may be driven by factors other than basic economic need, such as being the best provider in their industry. This type of business, illustrated by Michael, can be referred to as a *Market Driven Family Business*.

Why is this an issue for you and your family business? Simply this: If your business is a Lifestyle Family Business, rather than a Market Driven Family Business, all the time, money and energy that you pour into it may not be enough to see the enterprise through from one cycle of growth to the next. You need to ask yourself some hard questions about your ability to create, nurture, and grow your business in a manner that will ensure its success for the long term.

For example, does the business have the ability in its current state to provide, at a minimum, for the economic needs of the family? Consider these relatively straightforward questions to test yourself:

- Is your business a leader in the marketplace?
- Does your business routinely take steps to investigate, develop, and pursue product and service offerings that represent the emerging position of your industry?
- Are the key functions in your business staffed by individuals, family members or otherwise, who are fully qualified to do the job that they hold?
- Are your recruitment criteria for filling positions based on hiring the best person that you can find, regardless of whether they are a family member or not?
- Do you impose training and evaluation requirements to ensure that all staff members are qualified to do the job that they hold, including family members?
- Does your business employ the right number of staff members to effectively run the business without any unnecessary positions?
- Do you have the right structures in place to minimize tax erosion?

If you answered "yes" to all or most of these questions, chances are you are operating your business as an enterprise that is focused on being successful in the market in which you operate—a Market Driven Family Business.

If you answered "no" to all or most of these questions, chances are your business is best characterized as a Lifestyle Family Business, where the main focus is on providing for the economic needs of the family.

So here is the key issue: If your business is a Lifestyle Family Business, your investment in the family business may be at risk. Why? Without a definitive plan to grow revenues and/or maximize the equity already built in your business, you risk exposure to erosion from competitive forces, as well as taxes and inflation. However, if you are currently operating a Lifestyle Family Business and have a desire and/or need to move to the Market Driven Family Business approach, you may need to increase your knowledge and make decisions so that your business will continue to grow and develop.

THE SOLUTIONS

Making the shift from a Lifestyle Family Business to a Market Driven Family business is not an easy one, nor will it happen overnight. It requires an understanding of the key attributes of businesses that are competitive forces in the marketplace—those that provide and/or develop product or service offerings *that are driven by the needs and wants of customers*, as opposed to focusing on what is most convenient for the family. This will not happen without a plan.

Most businesses should have a business plan that outlines the goals, objectives, core activities and strategies, as well as projected financial results of the business for the next three to five years. At a minimum, a business should have an annual operating plan and budget that includes the goals and core activities for the year, as well as projected financial results. These documents, the details of which will not be considered here, are the starting point for developing a Business Transformation Plan to move the company to the Market Driven Family Business level.

The Business Transformation Plan

The Business Transformation Plan will provide the roadmap for moving a Lifestyle Family Business to a Market Driven Family Business. Using your existing business plan as a starting point, it will address many of the topics that are included in this book, including:

- Level of family involvement, in terms of roles and responsibilities and ownership
- Performance management requirements and expectations
- Strategy for involving non-family members
- Planning for succession, in terms of roles and responsibilities and transfer of the business
- Growth-oriented options, such as additional capital, partnerships, mergers, etc.

These key strategy and decision areas will be supported by the appropriate technical structure, such as share ownership, income splitting, family trusts, and estate freezes, which is critical in terms of developing a tax-effective approach and maximizing wealth for the family.

The suggested approach for building a Business Transformation Plan is to conduct a "gap" analysis in each of the key areas, whereby the current state of your business is documented in each area and compared to the desired state, as outlined in this book. The difference between the two situations (i.e., the "gap") is determined and action-oriented recommendations are developed to address the gap. This approach is helpful, as it will allow you to see and understand not only where your business requires modification, but will also provide a clear and action-oriented plan as to what the next steps should be. Depending on the extent and nature of the action plan steps, a timeline can also be developed.

The Business Transformation Planning Process

As a family business leader, you are not only the expert of your business, you are also an expert in terms of your family unit. This situation can result in challenging and sometimes conflicting perspectives, particularly since close family relationships are a significant part of the mix. You may recognize, after careful consideration, that a Lifestyle Family Business will no longer meet the economic needs of the family and you will have to shift to a market driven approach. This type of change can involve some difficult decisions that must be made in the best interest of the business, and ultimately, the family.

Facing this type of situation on your own cannot only be stressful, but the impact of personal relationships on decision making can ultimately result in the changes that need to be made not occurring, which will result in the business failing to evolve to the necessary competitive position, which puts the family's economic well-being at risk. In fact, the change that was meant to protect the future of the family's financial position can be undermined due to an attempt to protect family harmony in the short term.

A better approach to address the issue of moving towards a Market Driven Family Business is to engage an independent business advisor to guide the process. You may currently have someone in your advisory network that has the ability to fulfill this role, or you may wish to identify someone completely new to the situation. One of the benefits of a business advisor that is new to the situation is that they will typically bring a fresh perspective, and may identify issues or opportunities that someone who is already involved may not readily recognize. They can also bring the benefit of being truly independent, as they do not have any history with the business, family members, or existing advisors. Sometimes this type of objectivity can bring a new clarity and credibility to the situation.

Regardless, whoever you select as a business advisor to lead the business transformation process, they should have the necessary qualifications and an established track record in terms of business planning, financial management, and running a business. Knowledge and experience in the areas of change management, human resources, tax matters, and business financing (i.e., raising capital, business sale, acquisitions, etc.) is certainly helpful, as shifting to a Market Driven Family Business will include most, if not all, of these issues.

Once an advisor has been identified, meet with them to discuss your expectations, in terms of timelines, objectives, and how the advisor can best assist you during the process. Once this has been established, review and discuss your current business plan and start to identify the process for documenting your business's current state within each of the gap analysis areas. Also identify any areas where you feel you are lacking information to move forward. For example, you may wish to more fully understand the trends and areas of opportunity within your industry in order to confirm the ones you think your business should pursue. Your business advisor should be able to assist you with market research sources, by way of direct customer research, expertise to assist in this area, or organizations you could contact to obtain this type of information.

You are now ready to embark upon the process of developing a Business Transformation Plan that will assess the position of your business, as compared to the profile of a Market Driven Family Business, as well as provide an action plan for moving forward. Read on, as we discuss the key areas to understand, consider, and address.

IN SUMMARY

Family businesses should have a strategy for the future of the business in order to safeguard the family's most important asset for future generations.

Businesses that operate as Lifestyle Family Businesses focus on meeting the family's economic needs, and may not need to or wish to work beyond this level. Market Driven Family Businesses seek to respond to needs in the marketplace and can become the objective of a Lifestyle Family Business, particularly in terms of better positioning the business for the future.

Transforming a Lifestyle Family Business to a Market Driven Family Business is not an easy or quick achievement, and is best approached with a Business Transformation Plan that focuses on the key requirements to move the company forward, supported by the appropriate technical structure. A qualified business advisor can be helpful to guide the business transformation process.

THINGS YOU NEED TO KNOW

- Both Lifestyle and Market Driven Family Businesses can be successful and well regarded. The key issue is determining what approach is required to meet, and perhaps exceed, the family's economic needs, both now and in the future.

- Failing to determine if your business can meet the future economic requirements of the family and implementing the necessary business and tax strategies puts the family's well-being at risk.

- If you want your business to compete on a market driven level, you will have to first focus on what is necessary in order to do so, as opposed to first focusing on what is most convenient for the family. In terms of business decision making, what is in the best interest of the business should ultimately prevail.

QUESTIONS YOU NEED TO ASK

- Is my business a Lifestyle Family Business or a Market Driven Family Business?

- Am I satisfied with the category in which the business currently falls?

- Is the business currently meeting the financial needs of the family? What is the outlook for future years?

- If you want to move to the category of Market Driven Family Business, what could be some of the impacts to the family, both positive and negative?

- If the business continues to operate as a Lifestyle Family Business, what will it look like in 5 years', 10 years', and 20 years' time? Will it be able to provide for the family's economic needs? Will the business continue to exist?

- How would the family's economic needs be met if the business no longer existed?

THINGS YOU NEED TO DO

- Determine if you alone have the skills, time, and energy level to re-position the business.
- Determine if you currently have a qualified business advisor who could assist you in developing a Business Transformation Plan.
- Review the financial performance of the business for the last five years, paying careful attention to trends and profitability levels. Identify whether the business is in a state of growth, stability, or decline.
- Develop a high level forecast of the financial performance of the business for the next three to five years. Identify whether the business is expected to be in a state of growth, stability, or decline.
- Determine if additional capital is likely to be required, and if so, how it could be provided.

DECISIONS YOU NEED TO MAKE

- Determine if you need to or wish to take the necessary steps to move your business from a Lifestyle Family Business to a Market Driven Family Business.
- Select an independent business advisor(s) to assist you in the process.

MASTER YOUR INVESTMENT IN THE FAMILY BUSINESS
Entrepreneurial Spirit: Lifestyle vs. Market Driven Businesses

TIPS

- Focus on the business as a means of providing for the family's economic needs. Instead of thinking about family member personalities and relationships, think about the business as an engine. Consider things like its efficiency, how well it operates, and the type of performance (i.e., financial, tax, and other results) that it provides. Ask yourself if the existing engine is functioning the way that it should, or whether an overhaul is required before it stops working altogether.

- Think about what would happen if the business was not there; how would the family's economic needs be met? Consider the situation in terms of choosing between "the lesser of two evils" (i.e., significant changes to the business that may result in long-term survival and growth, as opposed to no changes being made, resulting in decline, wind down, or elimination of the business).

- Give yourself some time to think about the situation, recognizing that significant change does not happen overnight. Having said that, give yourself a reasonable time limit to decide what your course of action will be and then move to the next step.

TRAPS

- Focusing solely on family member personalities and circumstances has a good chance of leading to the wrong decision, or perhaps no decision at all. One of the complications with family businesses is that they involve close personal relationships, which can impact decision making. Making decisions based on the personal circumstances of family members can lead to decisions that are not in the best interest of the business.

- If you are serious about moving your Lifestyle Family Business to a Market Driven Family Business, do not go it alone. Chances are you will be faced with some challenging decisions, and may find yourself at odds with family members, at least for the short term. An experienced business advisor can keep the business transformation process on track, manage personalities, and provide you with an objective support and sounding board.

Principle Mastery: When a family business leader can make the distinction between positioning the business to capitalize on market opportunities to the benefit of the family, as opposed to solely structuring and running the business based on what is most convenient for family members, the basis exists for generating real wealth. Someone should reap the benefits of market opportunities—why not your business?

CHAPTER *2*

Family Involvement:
Share Ownership and the
Lifetime Capital Gains Exemption

An ounce of prevention is worth a pound of cure. BENJAMIN FRANKLIN

Sam and Rita are both in their late 50s. Over the last twenty years or so, they have built up a very successful niche manufacturing business with sales in excess of $5 million and pre-tax profits of roughly $500,000 each year. Their two children (Pam and Scott) are not actively involved in the business. Pam recently graduated as a nurse and Scott just entered law school.

Sam and Rita have always kept their business affairs and corporate structure fairly straightforward and simple. They are, however, starting to accumulate significant cash reserves in the company, as they have not been drawing out all of the profits they have generated over the last 10 years.

Sam recently attended the members' opening cocktail party of his golf and country club and was speaking with one of his golfing buddies who told him about selling his company and claiming the Lifetime Capital Gains Exemption. His buddy had boasted that they got several million dollars out tax free, thanks to the planning by his tax accountant.

Sam knew of the capital gains exemption, but made a mental note to follow this up with his financial advisors. He liked the idea of a few million dollars of tax-free money and wondered how his buddy had done that. Sam started thinking about whether there was something that he and Rita should do now to prepare for a sale.

THE ISSUES

Sam and Rita's long-term thoughts about their business assets are to maximize family wealth by selling their company to a larger competitor, or perhaps transitioning ownership by way of a sale to an employee group.

But in the meantime, Sam and Rita had other concerns they needed help with now. How could they protect themselves—and the cash assets they have built up in the company—from creditors or other claims that could arise if the company was sued? Also, Sam was increasingly concerned about the growing exposure his company had with the large box-stores he sold to in the U.S. What if there was a problem with his product or if someone got hurt using it? He really needed to do something to safeguard what he and Rita had worked so hard to build up. And he needed some sound advice to help with their decision making.

On referral from his golfing buddy, Sam made an appointment with a financial advisor who identified two key issues that Sam and Rita were facing:

1. Preservation of the value in their existing business.
2. Positioning of the business to take advantage of the $750,000 capital gains deduction.

Preservation of Value in the Existing Business

Since Sam and Rita have ploughed back the corporate earnings into the business, the value of the company has increased. Sam was right to be concerned about the safety of the cash and investment assets, which are at risk if the company is sued by a customer or if there is some claim resulting from a defect in the product. If the cash is not needed in the business, Sam and Rita need to find a way to remove it before any claim comes to fruition.

Positioning for the $750,000 Capital Gains Deduction

Sam and Rita need to position their corporate holdings to take advantage of the $750,000 Lifetime Capital Gains Exemption. This exemption is available to every individual resident in Canada who sells qualifying shares of a small business corporation. This means that even though their children, Pam and Scott, are not involved in the company, they would each be entitled to the $750,000 Lifetime Capital Gains Exemption if they, in fact, did own shares. There is no requirement for them to be actively involved in the company. If each of the four of them did own shares in the company, the entire family would benefit from $3 million of capital gains deductions, which would save the family around $750,000 in income taxes.

However, if Sam and Rita got a really good offer to sell their shares today, it is unclear whether the company would even qualify for the $750,000 Lifetime Capital Gains Exemption. That's because the rules for eligibility are very complicated. The fact that the company holds all that extra cash, which is not being used directly in the business, could put the company "offside" for purposes of the deduction.

Sam's financial advisor was not a tax specialist, but a seasoned advisor who really understood these issues. Wisely, he suggested that Sam and Rita consult a tax specialist to help them implement a plan to deal with these issues. Sam had a good accountant who put together his financial statements and compiled his taxes, but he had not consulted a tax specialist before. Things had always been pretty straightforward; however, Sam and Rita now realized the time was right to bring in an expert.

THE SOLUTIONS

Sam and Rita's meeting with the tax specialist was very enlightening. A number of alternative solutions were identified, yet it seemed like nothing was "black and white". The three of them spent time discussing two important solutions:

- The use of a holding company
- An "estate freeze" to a family trust

The Use of a Holding Company

Setting up a new holding company was one solution to properly position the investment in the business for both the preservation of existing value and a potential capital gains deduction for each family member. This would involve issuing common shares to all family members, including Pam and Scott, in the holding company. Sam and Rita would then transfer their shares of the operating company to the holding company. Fortunately, this transfer can be done on a tax-deferred basis, providing certain tax planning is implemented and tax elections are filed with CRA.

The goal of the new structure would be to have the children participate in the future growth of the business. As the business would increase in value, the shares of their holding company would also increase in value. Future capital gains realized on a sale or transfer of the business could then be split with their children, and each one of them could access their $750,000 Lifetime Capital Gains Exemption.

The holding company also provides the corporate vehicle in which excess cash assets and investments from their operating company can be transferred "up-stream" to their holding company. The transfer can occur by way of a *tax-free inter-corporate dividend*, because the operating company and the holding company would be considered to be "connected" corporations for tax purposes. That was great news for Sam and Rita!

The holding company also provides a degree of creditor-proofing and a safety net if the operating company is sued. Cash and investment assets not used directly in the operating company business can be transferred to the holding company, thereby removing the exposure these assets would have otherwise had.

However, the tax advisor pointed out certain concerns and limitations in using a holding company strategy:

- **Stacked Corporations.** Meeting the test of a "qualifying small business corporation" will become substantially more difficult when a business owner creates "stacked corporations" (i.e. when one company owns another, such as a holding company owning all the shares of an operating company, the structure is referred to as "stacked corporations"). When there is only one operating company, the shares of that company can qualify for the capital gains deduction if certain rules are met. Among these are:

a. The "24-month test". During the 24 months preceding a sale, the shares cannot be owned by anyone other than the taxpayer, the taxpayer's spouse or common-law partner, or a partnership related to the taxpayer, and 50% or more of the fair market value of the assets of that company must be used in an active business carried on primarily in Canada. Cash and investment assets not used directly in the business operations will not qualify and can actually "taint" the eligibility of the shares.

b. The "substantially-all test". At the actual time of the sale, all or substantially all of the assets (generally meaning 90% or more) of the company must be used in the active business of the company.

This 24-month test does not apply in respect of treasury shares issued to an individual in exchange for business assets transferred to the company, as part of a transaction to "incorporate" the business, provided that the particular business was carried on for a 24-month period by that individual. It also does not apply in respect of a properly structured estate freeze.

The test becomes much more onerous where there is a HOLDCO-OPCO structure. The 24-month test requires that at least one of the companies must meet the "substantially-all" test throughout the 24 months preceding the date of sale. If either company is "offside" for even one day, then the shares will not qualify for the $750,000 Lifetime Capital Gains Exemption and the owners must bring the asset mix back onside and wait another 24 months to qualify!

- **Liability Issues.** The advisor also pointed out that introducing their children as direct owners in the company (or indirectly through a holding company) may introduce other liability issues or even potential claims from future relationships which their children may enter. Sam nodded his agreement. This was important. He knew already that Pam had moved in with her partner once she earned her nursing degree and he wasn't too sure how the relationship would go.

Freeze to a Family Trust

A second solution involved the setting up of a discretionary family trust for the benefit of Sam and Rita's children and potentially their grandchildren. The tax advisor explained the advantages in using a family trust to achieve their long-term capital gains splitting objectives.

Because the trust separates "legal" from "beneficial" ownership, no one beneficiary has a vested right to the income or capital of the trust unless and until the trustees designate such income or capital to them. The trust acts as a conduit or "flow-through" and permits the tax treatment of income (including dividends and capital gains) to be afforded the same tax treatment as though such amounts were earned directly.

And, because there can be multiple beneficiaries, the use of the $750,000 Lifetime Capital Gains Exemption can be multiplied by as many times as there are beneficiaries.

However, because of the separation of "legal" and "beneficial ownership", a beneficiary would generally not have any claim to the underlying assets held by the trust. This therefore provides a degree of creditor-proofing and also a safeguard against claims from other persons who may be in a relationship with a family member.

This seemed to solve many of the concerns Sam and Rita had. But what would they need to do to set up the trust? The accountant explained the procedure carefully:

First, Sam and Rita would exchange their common shares for newly issued *fixed value preference shares*, which have a fair market value and redemption value equal to the fair market value of their "old" common shares. Once again, this exchange can occur on a tax-deferred basis.

Next, the newly created family trust would then subscribe and pay for nominal value common shares in the operating company.

Because Sam and Rita's share value was now fixed or "frozen", all future growth in the common shares would accrue to the benefit of the trust. The trust would be administered by a number of trustees and a written trust document would set out all governing terms and provisions, as well as powers afforded to the trustees.

In a discretionary trust, title of the new common shares would vest with the trustees, but beneficial ownership (including rights to income and capital) would belong to the beneficiaries. The tax advisor had suggested that beneficiaries be identified by "class", so that individuals who are born into the family (i.e. grandchildren) obtain a contingent or discretionary interest in the trust.

The tax advisor also suggested that there should be provision for a corporate beneficiary. The existence of another company would provide the opportunity to dividend out cash and investment assets from the operating company to the corporate beneficiary via the trust. The transfer of assets through a trust to a corporate beneficiary can also occur on a tax-deferred basis.

The ability to do so would ensure that there is no undue build-up of cash assets in the operating company and this approach also works to keep the company "onside" for purposes of the $750,000 Lifetime Capital Gains Exemption.

IN SUMMARY

This chapter focused on the structuring of the ownership in a family business to maximize the use of the $750,000 Lifetime Capital Gains Exemption and provides solutions for a variety of common risk management issues that usually come into play for a family-owned business.

The family business can easily be one of the largest assets owned. Proper and efficient tax planning is essential in order to maximize family wealth. To do so requires a proper corporate structure and ongoing monitoring to ensure that the company will qualify for the Lifetime Capital Gains Exemption when the opportunity to sell arises.

The tax consequences relating to a corporate restructuring, including the use of a holding company or a trust, are complex and a tax advisor who is familiar with this area of practice should be consulted well in advance of any planned sale or disposition.

THINGS YOU NEED TO KNOW

- As an owner in the family business, your shares probably represent a significant percentage of your net worth.
- You, and each and every family member, are entitled to the $750,000 Lifetime Capital Gains Exemption.
- The tests under the Income Tax Act to ensure that the shares of the family business qualify are complex: There is a 50% "24-month test", a 90% "substantially-all test" at the date of sale and a more complicated "anti-stacking test" where you have a HOLDCO-OPCO structure.
- Introducing children/grandchildren as direct shareholders in the company can be problematic in that it may introduce new risks.
- A family trust is an excellent means to multiply the $750,000 Lifetime Capital Gains Exemption. The trust also can provide flexibility and creditor-proofing for the family as a whole.

QUESTIONS YOU NEED TO ASK

- What is our company worth today?
- Do the shares qualify for the $750,000 Lifetime Capital Gains Exemption?
- When do we plan to sell?
- How much tax will we have to pay if we sold today? (Do we know whether the Lifetime Capital Gains Exemption applies?)
- Is it likely that our children or employees will want to buy the company?

THINGS YOU NEED TO DO

- Assess the current estimated value of your company.
- Identify tax strategies to minimize tax on a future sale (or transfer to other family members).
- Review the corporate structure with a view to maximizing overall family wealth.
- Review your personal tax situation and assess eligibility to claim the $750,000 Lifetime Capital Gains Exemption.

DECISIONS YOU NEED TO MAKE

- Determine whether you should restructure corporate holdings.
- Consider implementing a family trust.
- Consider the use of a holding company.

MASTER YOUR INVESTMENT IN THE FAMILY BUSINESS

Family Involvement: Share Ownership and the Lifetime Capital Gains Deduction

TIPS

- Act sooner rather than later. When an offer emerges, it may be too late to restructure and fix an "offside" structure. If you have to wait 24 months before the shares qualify again, the buyer will likely have moved on.

- Assess current values for the family company. An untimely death or disposition could result in an unexpected capital gains tax. For this reason, it would be prudent for the company to carry adequate life insurance to fund an unexpected tax liability.

- Review your will to ensure that you understand the tax consequences that can arise on a transfer of property occurring on death. While a transfer to a spouse or spousal trust occurs on a tax-deferred rollover basis, a transfer to your children will not. Such a transfer could trigger an unexpected capital gains tax.

- Seek competent tax advice. The matters are complex.

TRAPS

There are a few new tax terms family business owners need to master to fully maximize their tax-free capital gains on the sale or transfer of their business:

- Ask your tax specialist about CNIL. The cumulative net investment loss (CNIL) rules can prevent you from claiming the capital gains exemption on the sale or disposition of your qualifying small business corporation's shares. CNIL can arise where you have borrowed money and deducted interest on funds advanced to your company. Review your tax filings with your accountant prior to closing on a sale.

- Find out about the Alternative Minimum Tax ("AMT"). This provision can apply to create taxes owing in the year of sale. AMT arises because of a special tax calculation which excludes tax preference items, such as the $750,000 Lifetime Capital Gains Exemption.

Principle Mastery: When family business owners properly structure their affairs surrounding the ownership of their business asset, significant long-term wealth can be built for current and future generations. It pays to get specialized tax advice in advance.

CHAPTER 3

Family Involvement: Planning for Participants and Bystanders

When the bloom is off the rose. TRADITIONAL SAYING

Mary Ann started a floral design business 11 years ago with the goal of supporting herself and her two young children. Recently divorced, Mary Ann needed to create an income, a challenge, since she had been a stay-at-home mother for a number of years. Her children, Allison and Matthew, now aged 20 and 18, watched her build the business from a part-time initiative, developed from Mary Ann's enthusiasm for floral design courses taken in the evenings at a local community college, to a bustling enterprise employing 15 staff members in both a retail shop and an online delivery service.

Over the years, Mary Ann had spent a considerable number of hours building the business, with her days consumed by meeting with customers and talking to suppliers, and evenings with administrative and bookkeeping tasks. It was not unusual for her to have to set aside piles of order forms to help her children with their homework, or for business calls to interrupt the dinner hour. Mary Ann was the heart of the business, its driving force, and not a single flower arrangement would go out the door without her stamp of approval.

As the business continued to grow, bringing increased challenges with every new customer, Mary Ann needed some help. She had plenty of staff members to do the front line work, but felt overwhelmed by the growing administrative, management, and supervision responsibilities. She thought that getting her children involved in the business was an obvious solution, as she would like nothing more than be able to "duplicate herself" with someone who would bring the same attention to detail that she does, as well as provide a trustworthy resource that would instinctively know how she would like things to be done.

Mary Ann considered Matthew, in his first year of university in management studies, less likely to become involved. Allison, currently studying interior design, would be well suited to join the business, and although she had never expressed an interest, Mary Ann considered her to be a natural fit. Help in sight—what a relief!

THE ISSUES

Mary Ann's story is not an unusual one; a business starts out of economic necessity and experiences growth beyond the expectations or capacity of the founder. Years go by, characterized by the grind of meeting the daily requirements of the business and trying to fulfill family obligations. Although most business owners do their best to maintain some aspect of control and balance, it is not uncommon for business and family obligations to blend together into one big 24-hour blur, day after day.

Even though they were not active in the business, the business was very much present in the lives of Mary Ann's children, who saw their mother strive to complete all of the business tasks she needed to accomplish in a day from the time they were very young. Their lives were interrupted when the business needed attention, and whether Mary Ann realizes it or not, her children have likely long since formulated their own opinions of the business, their degree of interest in it, and what an even closer relationship with it could mean to their futures. *Chances are, she does not have a good grasp on this issue, and perhaps, like many business owners, she has been too busy building the business to think about it.*

The problem is this: Mary Ann has not taken the steps to build in the depth necessary to successfully transition her Lifestyle Family Business to a Market Driven Family Business and has now overextended herself. The growth of the business is constrained by what she alone can accomplish in a management capacity, and this could result in missed revenue opportunities, substandard customer service, and decreased product quality, all of which represent risks to the success and value of the business. Further, she really has done nothing to actively mentor her perceived successor, and there is no evidence of her children's interest in the role, beyond her own expectations. In fact, it may now be too late to build that link.

Mary Ann has two challenges to consider:

Family member involvement/business succession is likely not an option. Since their mother has not engaged them in a discussion process about their possible involvement in the business, Mary Ann's children have not had an opportunity to learn firsthand about the business and the opportunities it presents. They may even have assumed that she has other plans and directed their interests elsewhere. Besides, the business has been a high maintenance, deeply resented, and unwelcome family member!

No formal growth/succession plan. Mary Ann in fact does not have a formal growth or succession plan; she has been practicing little more than "imaginary succession" —clearly a risk to the future of the business—and she has not taken steps to explore and develop alternate succession options, given the apparent lack of interest from her family members.

The issues for Mary Ann to think about, preferably with the help of professional advisors, include the following:

- What is the growth plan for the business in the foreseeable future?
- Is the involvement of one or both of her children the best option for the future growth of the business?
- Are they suited to and interested in becoming involved in the business?
- How will involvement of one child, but not the other, affect the siblings?
- How will this impact the dynamics within the family unit as a whole?

THE SOLUTIONS

What could Mary Ann have done differently to avoid this type of situation?

You need a Business Transformation Plan. The first step is to recognize that having a plan for growth and succession of the business and replacing senior level managers—including the business leader—is required to support the growth of a Market Driven Family Business. This is a critical component of a family business continuation strategy.

But, in order to transition from a Lifestyle Family Business to a Market Driven Family Business, a formal Business Transformation Plan is required. In the case of family businesses, looking first to family members to fulfill the growth and succession roles is common. However, in order to be effective, family business leaders need to do more than simply hire those within the family unit to carry on the business.

You need to mentor future leaders with vision. The second step is to recognize that one of the simplest and most effective things that a family business leader can do to engage family members is to talk to them about the business. Although this is a very straightforward thing to do, it is not uncommon for all of the emphasis to be placed on running the business and meeting its operational needs, as opposed to actually talking about the vision for the business' future in a way that engages the interest of family members. When people can participate in the future, feelings of resentful exclusion, as well as a poor understanding of what the business is actually about can give way to an understanding of opportunities for involvement and the skills that are required for the privilege of being involved.

To master the investment in the family business, there is much family business leaders can do to mentor their successors in a positive way.

Communicate the Business Basics

The first step is to provide family members with a basic understanding of the business, covering specific topic areas:

- **Mission and vision.** What is the potential for the future of the business? What are the guiding principles and strategic plans of the business's management team to get there? What are the goals and objectives of the business in terms of navigating the path to its destination?

- **Main functions of the business.** What industry is it in? What are the products and/or services that it offers?

- **Markets and customers.** Who are the customers of the business? What are some of the important issues faced by customers of the business? What is the customer service philosophy?

- **Roles in the business.** What are the main departmental areas within the business? What are the types of jobs within the business? What key skills are required by the business? What are the requirements for training, professional development, and advancement within the firm?

- **Role in the community.** What is the business leader's vision for corporate citizenship within the community? What philanthropic efforts, volunteerism, and community accomplishments are a part of the company's soul and spirit?

- **Future expansion plans.** Where is the business at today, and what are some of the future plans for the business (i.e., additional locations, new product lines, acquisitions, partnerships, etc.)?

- **The difference between family business succession and family wealth succession.** There is a difference between the ongoing nurturing and growth of the family business and stewardship of the family wealth. Family members need to understand the difference, and business leaders need to provide clarity around the issues of entitlement.

Providing this basic information gives family members a friendly introduction to the heart and soul of the business, its functions, customers, and the various roles within the enterprise. Family members will gain an understanding of the role of the business within the community and what makes it successful, and will likely feel some pride when important accomplishments, like a new location or big contract, occur.

Instead of regarding the business as an unknown entity that is thrust upon them, family members will be more likely to feel like they are actually part of the business and the team that makes it a success. They will also begin to understand that the business and its successful functioning provides for the family's economic needs, which is worthy of safeguarding and respect.

More important, they may begin to see the vision for its future potential, and perhaps become part of the dream for the future, which may include a unique, impactful role.

Understanding Roles and Responsibilities

Communicating the key roles and positions within the business is important in terms of enabling family members to understand and relate to the human aspect of the business, as well as visualizing themselves taking on a role in the business.

Most of us can probably think of the ineffective son, daughter, or other family member who is employed in a family business, with no meaningful position, knowledge, or ability to assist in its operation; their sole credential is being a family member.

Too often there is only a vague understanding of "people that work for Dad", without any notion of the skills and experience they bring to the business. Instead of the children adopting a foregone conclusion that "when I grow up, I will work in the business with Mom or Dad", they will come to understand and take it upon themselves to acquire the knowledge and skills to do the job and, at this point, their potential contribution can be purposefully explored.

In the case of Mary Ann, her daughter Allison may come to the conclusion that the design aspect of the business is too narrow to suit her interests and may prefer to embark on a career with an interior design firm in order to achieve a higher level of variety, whereas Matthew may actually be attracted to the management aspect of the business, less interested in the actual industry, and see a good opportunity to gain practical management skills.

By providing an understanding of the jobs that are part of the business and what each individual brings to the success of the firm, family members can start to gauge their level of interest in terms of fulfilling one of those roles, as well as the skills and experience that are necessary to successfully perform the job. They may even be mentored by a key employee.

Setting Expectations and Options

The extent to which expectations are set regarding the required skills and knowledge to hold a key position within the business can be the difference between a successful family business and a failed enterprise— it can be that simple.

It is the responsibility of the family business leader to provide a clear indication of the necessary qualifications, particularly for senior level positions, in terms of whether specialized education and training are required, or whether simply being a family member is sufficient. The latter, although not recommended, may be sufficient for a Lifestyle Family Business; however, the former is a key requirement for building a Market Driven Family Business.

Since the goal of a Market Driven Family Business is to successfully compete based on the needs of the marketplace, each job must be staffed by a person, family member or otherwise, with the necessary skills and experience to successfully perform the job; anything less than that decreases the likelihood that the business will be able to successfully compete in the marketplace, thereby putting the business and the family's wealth at risk. Once this fact is communicated and consistently reinforced to family members, it should have the effect of putting the requirements of the business first, to the benefit of the family, as opposed to focusing on individual family member situations.

Remember, the goal is for the business to create sustainable wealth for the family; this cannot be done with an unqualified management and staff group.

Once the family business leader has provided family members with an understanding of the business, the types of roles within the business, and the expectations regarding job qualifications, family members will be in a better position to make a decision as to whether or not they have an interest in working in the business on a day-to-day basis or assuming a passive role in the business.

Making the Decision

Given that family members have been engaged in a process to understand the business and their potential for involvement, one that ideally occurs over a number of years, they should ultimately have the necessary information to make a decision about their involvement.

Should family members not have an interest in working in the business, including succession of the enterprise, it is important for the family business leader to find this out sooner rather than later so that alternate strategies can be developed. Remember that the goal is to ensure that a Market Driven Family Business has the appropriate depth to enable and support growth, especially at the senior level. If engagement of and ultimate succession to family members is not an option, business owners may find themselves in Mary Ann's tenuous situation—leading a successful business with little more than an imaginary succession plan.

Family members should be empowered to make their own decision, as this will decrease the likelihood of feeling pressured into a situation that is not of their own choosing. They should understand that if they opt to have a day–to-day role in the business, it will mean that they will have a direct role in the business's success or failure, have input into decision making, and be compensated for their efforts, by way of salary, bonuses, ownership, or a combination thereof. Their compensation may be directly impacted by the performance of the business and their role in achieving that performance.

There should also be clarity for those who opt to be passively involved. They need to understand that they will not have significant input or responsibility in terms of how the business is run, will not draw salary or similar compensation, and may be limited to dividends and distributions as seen fit by those who run the business. This is important.

Addressing Financial Issues

Once the expectations for family involvement in the business have been set and understood, family business leaders will need to address how to implement the new roles of family members from a financial and structural perspective. This is where the help of professional advisors is critical.

The business may require a formal valuation and a new share ownership structure may be contemplated to enable the financial involvement of both active and passive family members on a fair and equitable basis. What's important is that business succession and family wealth succession are considered separately. Possible approaches could include:

- An estate freeze, enabling actively involved family members to participate in the future growth of the business by owning a portion of the existing business.
- Opportunities may exist to create a new company or division that the family member(s) could have the responsibility for developing and growing.
- Another option could be structuring an agreement where a portion of the company could transfer to the family member(s) at some future point in time.

All of these types of structures, which can be developed by a qualified advisor, have the benefit of focusing the family member's efforts on building the business and contributing to its financial results, as opposed to simply collecting a salary.

This type of approach is of particular importance in terms of building a Market Driven Family Business, as it emphasizes generating success in the marketplace, as a means to maximize financial results.

A final note on those family members who may opt not to be involved in the business on a day-to-day basis: Because people may have their own personal goals and objectives, this is completely understandable, and should be treated as such. Instead of dwelling on disappointment and other negative feelings, the leader of a Market Driven Family Business should appreciate having the knowledge and focus on what is best for the business, and family members should be told that their decision is respected. If the objective is to generate wealth for the family, this is best achieved by having qualified, competent, and motivated individuals in the business, as opposed to a reluctant family member.

However, in order to eliminate the "free ride" scenario, where uninvolved family members are given a token salary in exchange for little to no participation in the business, wealth may be transferred to uninvolved family members in other ways—for example, by sprinkling tax effective dividends or other distributions, perhaps from a family trust. This approach is consistent with the original objective of providing wealth to the family, without blurring the lines of day-to-day involvement versus passive involvement, and should be considered in detail with professional advisors, as discussed in Chapter 2.

Impact in Terms of Building a Succession Plan for a Market Driven Family Business

It is much easier to plan the succession of a Market Driven Family Business than a Lifestyle Driven one—the emotion is removed and the focus is on what's right for the business as an entity separate from family dynamics. The benefits are enormous:

- A family business leader will know where family members stand in terms of active or passive involvement in the business and can strategize accordingly.

- Family members will know the options for involvement and have been empowered to make a choice, which should minimize resentment and enable family members to take a leadership role in terms of the impact they can make in the business.

- Since the expectations and requirements for involvement are clear and consistent, family members will know what is required if they change their mind, and can take steps to gain the necessary knowledge and skills to join the business at some future point in time.

The overall focus is on what is best for the business, a key requirement for building and managing a Market Driven Family Business. In addition, family members will understand the business, options for involvement, and will have made their own choice of which path to pursue. They will also be aware of what changes they will have to make, should they wish to move to the other path. Personal empowerment and understanding of the business and the choices at hand should lead to respect for the business and the various roles that family members can choose to take, as well as increased harmony around the dinner table.

IN SUMMARY

Family businesses can grow from hard work and dedication, which all too often results in a situation where the family business leader has not planned to support the growth and succession needs of the business. Family members are captive bystanders in the process, and without being engaged in a communication process to understand the business and opportunities for involvement, they may opt out of participating, which results in the family business leader losing an obvious growth and succession option.

Engaging family members in a clear and consistent communication process about the business, key roles and responsibilities, and options for their involvement provides the information for family members to make an informed decision regarding active or passive involvement. The expectations that the family business leader sets, in terms of required skills, knowledge, and education to hold roles in the business represent a key determinant in terms of the level at which the business will operate in the marketplace. In the case of a Market Driven Family Business, requiring all individuals, family or otherwise, to have the necessary skills and experience to successfully perform the job is a must.

THINGS YOU NEED TO KNOW

- A growth and succession plan is a key component for a Market Driven Family Business, as well as the Business Transformation Plan, in the case of businesses migrating away from operating as a Lifestyle Family Business.

- Do not assume that family members will automatically join the business, succeed you as family business leader, or manage the business in the same manner in which you do. This is practicing imaginary succession.

- Family members benefit from information about the business, its functions, and the roles and responsibilities within the business. A good communication process helps them to make an informed decision as to their level of interest in terms of working in the business on a day-to-day basis.

- The objective of engaging family members in a discussion process about the business should not be to coerce them into taking an active role. The goal should be to provide information, assess the level of interest, and to make a decision in terms of day-to-day or passive involvement. Once this decision is made, you will have information as to whether alternate growth and succession planning steps are required.

- The focus should be on what is best for the business, with the goal of it operating as a Market Driven Family Business and providing wealth for the family. The best approach for success is to create a business of qualified, competent, motivated people, as opposed to one of reluctant family members. You need to be organized to compete against the best of the marketplace in order to achieve long-term success.

QUESTIONS YOU NEED TO ASK

- Have I engaged my family members in a communication process about the business?
- Do I make assumptions that family members will join the business?
- Have family members expressed interest (i.e., either active or passive) regarding the business?
- Have I communicated expectations regarding necessary qualifications to take an active role in the business?
- Do I have a formal growth and succession plan for the business, or have I been practicing imaginary succession?

THINGS YOU NEED TO DO

- If you do have a formal growth and succession plan for the business, review it to ensure that it is still current and that it has been developed with the objective of maintaining and growing a Market Driven Family Business, to create long-term wealth for the family.
- If you have not engaged family members in a discussion process about the business, it is time to start. Follow the guidelines of this chapter and develop an outline to start a dialogue with family members.
- If family members have indicated that they do not have an active interest in the business, you need to move forward with an alternate growth and succession plan, if you have not already done so.

DECISIONS YOU NEED TO MAKE

- Formulate your expectations as to the necessary qualifications for family members to join the business on a day-to-day basis. You need to decide if your approach is to staff each position with fully qualified and competent individuals to do the job, or whether simply being a family member is qualification enough. Remember, the leaders in the marketplace are the direct competitors for a Market Driven Family Business, and if you want your business to be successful, you need people who can get the job done.

- If family members have indicated an interest to join the business on a day-to-day basis, you need to decide if they possess the necessary skills and experience to successfully perform the job, or whether additional training or education is required. If so, this should be communicated to the family member.

MASTER YOUR INVESTMENT IN THE FAMILY BUSINESS

Family Involvement: Planning for Participants and Bystanders

TIPS

- Once again, focus what is best for the business, as opposed to focusing on family member situations. Remember, putting the success of the business at risk puts the family's economic well-being and future at risk.

- The cost of "carrying" an unqualified family member or one who is not willing to gain the necessary skills and experience to perform a job by employing them in the business comes at the expense of the family. Simply put, it is too much to ask.

- Give family members a reasonable amount of time to make a decision, but don't delay. The family business leader needs an answer, so that an alternate growth and succession plan can be developed if necessary.

- Using an independent business advisor can be useful in developing the growth and succession plan. They can bring objectivity to the process and may be aware of individuals who can help take the business forward, in the event that family members do not have an interest in being actively involved.

TRAPS

- Do not be inconsistent in your expectations in terms of necessary skills and experience to hold a position in the business. Family members need to know that this is not negotiable, otherwise the business will suffer.

- Do not pass judgment in terms of active or passive involvement in the business. This will create "classes" within the family, and infers that one category is better than the other, leading to friction and resentment. Respect people's decisions to maintain family harmony, recognizing that passive involvement is still involvement.

- If family members have indicated that they do not wish to have an active involvement in the business, do not delay pursuing an alternate growth and succession plan.

Principle Mastery: Taking an active approach to introduce and educate family members about the business is a basic, but important strategy for assessing their level of interest in being involved in the day-to-day operations of the business. The goal should be to get an answer—to determine what the level of interest is—so that decisions can be made to guide family members into the right education and training opportunities, or to find and develop other options if family members are not interested. Either way, the business's future is protected.

CHAPTER 4

Performance Management: Setting Expectations for Working Family Members

Oops, I did it again. BRITNEY SPEARS

Lexie and her two older brothers work in her family's metal fabrication business. The Company was started by her grandfather, who has since retired, and Lexie's father, Russell, manages the business. The company has been highly successful for most of her life (Lexie is now 23). Both of her brothers pursued specialized education in the areas of engineering and industrial design, but Lexie never had much of an interest in school; she was more interested in playing tennis and spending time with her friends, a number of whom are from families with successful businesses.

When Lexie joined the business two years ago, her father needed someone to help him manage the office. Russell was spending an increasing amount of time travelling, so he did not have the time to deal with office matters and he believed that Lexie had the "people skills" to look after this area. Although she did not have a formal job title, Russell figured she would take on increased responsibilities as she became more acquainted with the business. Lexie agreed to start.

Lexie recently decided to play in an upcoming tennis tournament. She was spending more time practicing and less time in the office. Staff members were reluctant to say anything to Russell, but they were clearly feeling pressure from the lack of direction. They did not find Lexie to be particularly helpful, given that she did not have a background in accounting or management, so they did the best they could to resolve issues.

In particular, Kate, the company's accounting manager, was becoming increasingly frustrated from being "supervised" by someone who knew far less about the business than she did. She started looking for employment elsewhere. Kate was an excellent employee who had been with the business for seven years and would have been the logical choice to be promoted to oversee the office. She realized that unless Russell took steps to address Lexie's job performance, she was in a hopeless situation.

THE ISSUES

How many times have you heard this story? A family business employs a member of the family who does not have the necessary skills to perform the largely undefined role that they were given, to the detriment of staff members, customers, and business itself. Staff members are reluctant to raise the issue with the family business leader, and either find a way to cope with the situation, or seek alternate employment. The family business leader is either unaware of the problem, or has no idea how to correct the situation, given that it involves disciplining (or perhaps firing!) a family member. In the end, the business loses; good employees, customers, and even potential employees look elsewhere to have their business and/or employment needs fulfilled. And of course, the family's wealth ultimately suffers when the business is negatively impacted in the marketplace.

This is a significant problem. Consider the following negative impacts on the business due to "mis-employment" of family member:

Employees of the business performing at an average level. Those who meet the basic expectations of the job will not typically realize their potential to perform at a higher level when the business is accepting of less than average job performance by others (family members or otherwise). Why is this the case? Simply because it sends a message that it is acceptable to perform below the required level, so when given the choice, why perform at a higher level than necessary? This low level of performance is not sufficient to enable the business to successfully compete in the marketplace (i.e., at the level of a Market Driven Family Business), which represents an ultimate cost to the organization.

Members of the business performing at an above average level. The "stars" of the organization may become unmotivated to continue to perform at a high level when they see the business accepting performance at a less than average level. This situation may surprise some people, as high achievers are often regarded as operating at a high level of performance, regardless of the environment. This is not a given; in fact, this type of situation can be extremely frustrating for above-average performers, who initially want the business to take steps to correct instances of poor performance so that the organization can function at its best. If this does not occur, above average performers will feel that their efforts are not being appreciated or are taken for granted and will either decrease their level of performance to an average level to create "equity" or look for opportunities outside of the business. Either way, these are the type of individuals that the business does not want to lose, and their loss or diminished performance represents a significant cost to the company.

Potential new members of the business. When the business attempts to hire individuals to replace those that leave the business, they may find it more difficult to do so than anticipated. Potential new members of the business may become aware that if they join the company they would be reporting to an incompetent family member and high performing candidates may choose not to pursue an opportunity on this basis. It is not unusual for this type of information to be discussed in the business community, including amongst employment recruiters, candidates, and those who have dealings with the business. Once this type of reputation becomes established, it can be difficult to overcome. The impact of this situation is that the business will be left with a pool of average to weak candidates or an insufficient number of candidates.

Customers. Customers look to their suppliers and/or service providers to fulfill their needs in a competent and reliable manner for an acceptable price. No customer wants to deal with a company that cannot or will not meet their requirements. If a business does not have a competent management and employee group, they face the very real risk of losing customers to companies that are in a better position to meet customer needs. This type of situation represents a clear loss of wealth for the business and the family and will only get worse until corrected, as the stories of poor customer service and unmet needs spread throughout the marketplace.

All of these factors build on one another to create a situation where the market position of the business is seriously diminished; some businesses never recover from this type of situation. What may have started out as an "internal family matter", employing a low performing family member, has become a marketplace legend and has put the business itself in jeopardy.

THE SOLUTIONS

You may think that Lexie is solely to blame for this situation; however, she is only part of the problem. Russell has failed to do a number of things to put Lexie in a position where she had a reasonable chance of being successful, and failed to address the situation when it became truly unacceptable.

What steps could Russell have taken to prevent this situation from occurring?

To begin, family business leaders must:

- Engage family members in a communication process about the business as an entity;
- Set clear and consistent expectations in terms of skills, education requirements, and experience to perform the job;
- Provide family members with the opportunity to make a decision in terms of their level of interest in taking on an active role in the business.

While we do not know if Russell engaged his children in a communication process about the business, or whether his children were empowered to make a decision regarding active or passive involvement, there is one important aspect that seems apparent.

The scenario suggests that Russell did not set clear and consistent expectations for Lexie's role in the business. Lexie does not have any formal education or experience to manage the office, which is clearly a shortfall, given the nature of the role. She is poorly equipped to manage an office of administrative and accounting staff members, given that she does not have any management or accounting education or experience. Russell's failure to set the expectation that specific skills, education, and experience are required to successfully perform this type of role has put Lexie at a disadvantage from the start.

The solution is to follow the guidelines discussed in Chapter 3, Family Involvement: Planning for Participants and Bystanders, particularly in terms of providing clear and consistent expectations for the requirements of the job. In cases of poorly performing family members, family business leaders need to look to their own behavior and ask "Did the expectations that I set or failed to set create this situation? Am I the one who is at fault?" If so, this type of behavior cannot be repeated and the current situation must be corrected.

Employment Contracts and Policies

It is important for family members to recognize that joining any business is a serious undertaking; this includes the family business. As with any employee, family members should be put on contract to formally define their role with the business, as well as the terms, conditions, and arrangements of their involvement. An employment contract, or similar document, is useful for communicating all of this information to members of the business, so that they understand the role and the obligations of both the individual and the company. A qualified human resources professional or legal advisor can assist in preparing employment contracts for use in your business.

One of the issues that growing businesses face is the challenge of implementing the appropriate documentation, policies, procedures, and performance measurement tools in order to provide the necessary structure to support future growth. Implementation of employment contracts and other human resource policies not only protects the business, it also integrates a professional management approach into the enterprise and for the engagement of family members, which is a basic requirement for taking a Lifestyle Family Business to the level of a Market Driven Family Business.

Reasonable Compensation for the Job Performed

Compensation for a position should be based on the value of the job to the business. This can be assessed in terms of the complexity and degree of risk associated with the tasks and responsibilities of the job, as well as the level of expertise, knowledge, and education or training required to hold the position. It is common to develop a salary range for each position, which provides room for an individual's level of compensation to progress as they become more proficient at performing the job, as well as some flexibility to compensate at an appropriate level, based on the specific qualifications of an individual.

From a compensation perspective, it is not appropriate to compensate an individual at a level above the relative worth of the job, and this can be a particularly tempting situation when dealing with family members. If an appropriate and consistent compensation strategy is not applied across all jobs in the organization, it will result in certain positions being skewed from the norm, solely because they are held by family members. This is not equitable, nor is it helpful when the job is no longer held by a family member.

Consider the following approach for compensating family members:

- First, compensate family members for the position that they hold. Their compensation level in this regard should be consistent with the salary range for the position, as well as the family member's skills and qualifications.
- Next, compensate family members for their level of performance, in terms of the how well they perform the job as compared to

performance evaluation criteria (see Regular and Constructive Performance Feedback section below). This compensation can come in the form of bonuses, profit sharing, or other perks, and will be determined based on the level of performance achieved. Performance-based compensation can be divided into short-term or annual (i.e., bonuses, profit sharing, etc.) and long-term (i.e., stock options, etc.) components, with long-term components providing targets for an individual to work towards achieving over a period of greater than one year.

- Finally, family members may hold shares in the business or receive dividends or other distributions based on their role in the family, or agreements to take over the business at some point in time. This "compensation" is separate from the compensation related to holding the specific job, which typically includes salary, performance-based compensation, and perks and benefits.

Structuring compensation arrangements in this manner provides a clear understanding to family members, in terms of amounts and entitlements that pertain to holding and successfully performing a job, as opposed to ownership and/or investment related earnings. It also helps to level the playing field between family and non-family members, recognizing that everyone in the organization has both responsibilities and rewards that are directly related to holding a position. In addition, a clear indication of the fair value of the position is established, and this is particularly important for family members to understand.

Clear Job Responsibilities

The fact that Lexie joined the business without a formal job title and with the expectation that she would take on increased responsibility as she became more familiar with the business represents Strike Two for Lexie. She was only given the vague responsibility of overseeing the office, with no supervision or mentorship from her father in terms of what was required in the role and how to perform it, given that he was typically away from the office.

All positions should have a job description that clearly lists the main responsibilities of the position. Job descriptions should indicate whether the position has a lead, shared, or supporting responsibility for each task, as well as the necessary skills, experience, and education to hold the position. A job description provides a clear indication of what the job entails, and is a precursor for performance evaluation, which is discussed in the next section. It also provides clarity, in terms of how the various jobs within the organization relate to one another, as well as indicating which job is responsible for which tasks. This is particularly important, in terms of resolving disputes about who is responsible for a given task, as well as for identifying any tasks that have not been assigned.

Job descriptions can also include information about the compensation range for the position, as well as reporting relationships and interactions with other positions in the organization. This information is useful in terms of understanding how the various roles within the organization interact, as well as identifying possible promotion and advancement opportunities.

One of the primary benefits of a comprehensive job description is that it clearly communicates to members of the business exactly what is required of them in terms of the tasks and responsibilities that they are required to perform in a particular job. It is also a useful tool for recruitment, as it provides the level of education, skills, and experience to select appropriate candidates and screen out those who do not qualify, as well as the compensation range for the position. Templates and guidelines for developing job descriptions are readily available on the Internet, in human resource publications, and from a qualified business advisor.

One of the things you may notice when you first attempt to develop job descriptions for the positions in your organization is that some of the information will come very easily, while other areas will require a fair amount of thought. This is particularly true when determining exactly how some functions that are shared by various positions are addressed, as well as determining which position is the most appropriate to perform a given task. If you are confused just thinking about it, imagine how confused members of the business are in the absence of this valuable information.

Regular and Constructive Performance Feedback

Regular and constructive performance feedback is an important aspect of a business that strives to compete successfully in the marketplace. A Market Driven Family Business wants to ensure that it is always putting its best foot forward, and an important component of this is ensuring that all jobs within the organization are being competently performed. When a business focuses on what it needs to do in order to be successful in the marketplace, it does not matter if the position is held by a family member or a non-family member. What matters is that the job is being done effectively, otherwise the business, and ultimately the family, suffers.

Performance feedback can include informal and formal aspects. Informal performance feedback is conducted on an ongoing basis, and can be as simple as a manager congratulating a staff member for a particular job task or situation (i.e., resolving a customer problem) that was well done. Conversely, when a member of the business has difficultly with a particular situation, or a problem arises, it is most effectively addressed at that time, so there is an immediate understanding of what they did wrong and how to better address the situation in the future. Informal performance feedback allows members of the business to know where they stand in terms of job performance, at any point in time, and takes the "surprise" element out of performance evaluation. People also take comfort in knowing that if there is a problem, it will be brought to their attention in a timely and constructive basis, instead of being stockpiled for confrontation at some future point in time.

Formal performance feedback usually takes the form of a performance evaluation, conducted at least once per year (many businesses have performance evaluation sessions twice per year). Formal performance evaluations are based on rating business member performance of the job tasks and responsibilities based on predetermined criteria. The job description should provide the basis for the areas in which performance is evaluated, as it includes a list of tasks and responsibilities that make up the job. This approach allows members of the business to understand the tasks and responsibilities upon which they are being evaluated, and provides the link between areas of responsibility and job performance.

It is a typical approach to score performance in each area on a numeric scale (i.e., a scale of 1 to 5, for example), supported by written comments to provide further explanation. The combination of numeric ranking and qualitative comments provides members of the business with tangible feedback, as well as some context for the ranking. This type of approach also requires the evaluator to think about their assessment in a structured and thorough manner.

An evaluation scale could have the following categories:

5 Consistently exceeds the requirements of the position in this area; employee is ready to take on more senior tasks/responsibilities

4 Generally exceeds the requirements of the position in this area; employee performs at an above average level

3 Meets the requirements of the position in this area; employee performs at an average level

2 Does not consistently meet the requirements of the position in this area; has a basic understanding of the requirement, but is not performing at a satisfactory level

1 Does not meet the requirements of the position in this area

Performance evaluations should include an action plan of items to be achieved within a specified period of time. An action plan can be developed for those who require improvement, as well as for high performing members of the business, in terms of setting targets for enhanced responsibilities and promotions.

Although performance feedback involves an assessment of how well the individual in the position is performing the job, it need not be overly "personal". It will be helpful to family business leaders to consider the needs to the business and what is required for the organization to perform at level of a Market Driven Family Business, as opposed to dwelling on personal circumstances. It is a reasonable expectation that most people do not come to work to be an ineffective member of the business, so the goal is to address job performance constructively and determine how performance can be improved. This could involve additional training, education, or perhaps assignment to another position in the business. Although not all performance issues can be successfully resolved, a well-defined performance feedback program can address many issues for the benefit of the business as a whole.

Addressing Training and Professional Development Requirements

It is important to recognize that most of today's successful businesses are learning organizations. This means that there is a culture and requirement for all members of the business to continue to gain knowledge and update their skills. Ongoing training and professional development can take a variety of formats including seminars, conferences, in-shop training sessions, courses, and professional designations. Opportunities exist for businesses to cover the costs of employee training and professional development and deduct the costs for income tax purposes. Ongoing professional development programs paid for by the employer can be useful recruitment tools for attracting above-average performers, as this type of individual often has a high degree of interest in professional development and advancement opportunities.

As previously mentioned, formal performance evaluations may include an action plan of items for achievement by a certain point in time. Identifying specific professional development requirements, such as completing an accounting designation in order to be considered for a promotion, can be a useful approach in maintaining a high level of job performance, as well as implementing a professional development program. It can also be used in instances of below average performance, as additional training and knowledge will provide, in most cases, the tools to improve, leaving the rest up to the individual. This approach provides a family business leader with the knowledge that they have taken the necessary steps to provide each individual with the opportunity to perform at an acceptable level, and if it is not successful, they will be able to move decisively to the next step, with the best interest of the business in mind.

Transfer and Termination

Unfortunately, not all hiring decisions are successful ones; this is the case for both employees and family members. A Market Driven Family Business is characterized by an environment that focuses on competing successfully in the marketplace by requiring above-average performance within the business. From a human resource perspective, this includes implementing, at a minimum, clear job descriptions, regular and constructive performance feedback, and a training and professional development program. This approach will raise the likelihood of successful staffing decisions and job performance, but will not eliminate every problem.

When it comes to hiring family members, it is absolutely critical to discuss termination at the time the family member is hired and to think through with that person how this would play out, both in terms of the business and family environment. This is a pre-emptive strike that is important in all hirings, but one that can be particularly important in terms of the context of family life.

Despite an enabling environment, family business leaders need to take immediate and decisive steps when family members just don't fit in the business. Options for resolving the situation could involve

- Moving the individual to another position or department within the organization for which they are better suited;
- Terminating the relationship altogether.

A transfer should not occur simply to "move the problem"; rather, it should only be done in situations where there is a high likelihood that the individual will be successful in the new position. This should be thoroughly considered by way of an assessment process, including reviewing the job description, training needs and professional development requirements with the individual to ensure that the requirements are consistent with the candidate's qualifications and capability. This type of process can be conducted with the assistance of a qualified human resources professional or business advisor.

Where there are no other reasonable options, unacceptable job performance should not be tolerated by the business, whether an employee or family member is involved. Termination of the relationship should occur, utilizing the best practices for doing so, including the following:

- Ensure that formal performance evaluations and incidences of unacceptable performance/behavior, if applicable, are documented in writing.

- If attempts to improve job performance, such as coaching, training, and professional development are not successful, termination should occur on a timely basis.

- The individual's direct supervisor/manager should typically be the one to conduct the termination in a meeting specifically set for this purpose.

- It is helpful for the meeting to be attended by a qualified human resources professional, either employed by the business or external, to address the individual's administrative and personal requirements after the manager has completed the termination and left the meeting.

- A letter confirming the termination and related arrangements should be provided to the individual during the meeting. Preparation of termination letters can be done by a qualified human resources professional or legal advisor.

- Once the termination has been completed, the members of the business should be immediately informed of its occurrence and the focus should be on how responsibilities will be transitioned or fulfilled. It is helpful to assure members of the business that the focus is on going forward, in a positive and constructive manner.

- Once an individual has been terminated, they should be allowed to briefly collect their personal effects and then leave the premises.

- Severance packages should be paid according to appropriate practice.

- An "outplacement" service provided by a qualified human resources firm can be helpful in terms of moving the terminated employee forward (that is, with resume preparation, counselling, networking, etc.).

The focus should always be on what is in the best interest of the business and the people who work in it, which means creating and maintaining an effective management and staff group, family members or otherwise.

It may be intimidating to think about the prospect of terminating a family member, but instead, think about all of the things that could have been done to avoid getting to this point, including:

- Engaging family members in a communication process about the business, in terms of its functions, customers, and key roles in the organization
- Setting clear and consistent expectations of the required skills, knowledge, and experience to hold a particular position
- Allowing family members to make an informed decision in terms of whether they wish to take an active or passive role in the business
- Using employment contracts for all members of the business, outlining the role, terms and conditions, compensation, and obligations of both the individual and the company
- Providing clear job responsibilities by way of a job description, that includes required tasks, qualifications, relationship to other jobs in the organization, and compensation arrangements for the position
- Providing regular and constructive performance feedback, particularly in terms of areas requiring improvement and an action plan for resolution
- Creating a learning environment through training and professional development to address performance shortfalls and provide the required knowledge for promotion, advancement, and new experiences

When a family business leader provides all of the necessary support and guidance to enable a family member to make a good decision as to their involvement in the business and identifies a role that is well-suited to their skills and interests where they can be successful, they have a winning situation. Anything less than that simply is not fair to the business, which means that the best place for a low-performing family member is on the sideline in a passive role.

IN SUMMARY

Family business leaders need to understand how to set guidelines for the various roles in the enterprise, evaluate performance, provide career enhancement opportunities, and address performance shortfalls. This is true in the case of all members of the business, whether they are family or non-family members.

It is important to recognize that a family member performing poorly in a position may not be the only one at fault. The family business leader may have failed to set consistent expectations in terms of the necessary qualifications to perform the job, have arbitrarily put a family member in a position that does not match their skills, or provided little guidance as to the tasks and responsibilities of the job. These types of problems can be addressed by way of employment contracts, appropriate compensation, job descriptions, regular and constructive performance feedback, and training and professional development programs.

In the case of a situation that cannot be salvaged, it may be necessary to terminate the employment of a member of the business. It is important to recognize that, in most cases, there are a number of things that can be done to avoid reaching this point, and while it is up to the business to provide the tools to improve performance, it is ultimately up to the individual to make it happen.

THINGS YOU NEED TO KNOW

- If a family member is performing poorly in a job, they may not be solely to blame for the situation. It is possible that consistent expectations in terms of the necessary qualifications and requirements to hold a position in the business were not set by the family business leader.

- Customers will not continue to be loyal to your business in times of below average service and quality. If there are better performers in the marketplace (i.e., including the Market Driven Family Businesses), chances are your business will start to lose customers.

- It is possible to create an environment for good job performance. Clear expectations, in terms of roles and responsibilities, compensation, performance feedback, training and professional development resources, and opportunities for advancement can empower all members of the business, family or otherwise, to be successful.

QUESTIONS YOU NEED TO ASK

- Have I provided clear and consistent expectations to family members in terms of the qualifications and requirements for roles in the business?

- Have I provided guidance and mentorship to help family members become acquainted with the business and their role?

- Does the business use employment contracts for all individuals actively involved in the company?

- Does the business provide clear information in terms of the tasks, responsibilities, and qualifications for each position by way of job descriptions?

- Does the business provide regular performance feedback, including performance evaluations and an action plan for improvement?

- Is the business a learning environment, in terms of promoting training and professional development opportunities and requirements?

- Are family members being compensated at a level that is reasonable for the particular position that they hold?
- Are there some members of the business that are not performing well and have steps been taken to address the issue?

THINGS YOU NEED TO DO

- Review the current human resources practices and systems in your organization and take steps to improve the human resource aspect of your business. This is useful for all family businesses and is an important component of the Business Transformation Plan.
- Schedule a meeting with a qualified human resources professional to discuss how your business is currently performing. Inquire as to the types of services that they provide and what steps might assist in improving the human resource function of your business.
- If there are members of your business that are not performing as required, you need to take steps to resolve the situation. Waiting or hoping that the situation will resolve itself is not effective and can actually harm the business.

DECISIONS YOU NEED TO MAKE

- Determine how the necessary human resource requirements will be implemented in your business.
- Determine whether to engage a qualified human resource professional to add credibility to the process, if your company is large enough to warrant a full-time human resource manager.

MASTER YOUR INVESTMENT IN THE FAMILY BUSINESS

Performance Management: Setting Expectations for Working Family Members

TIPS

- Members of the business who are well-directed, trained, and motivated will perform well. An effective and well-performing staff and management group is a significant resource for any business.

- It is important to be consistent in terms of implementing and maintaining human resource policies and procedures. Members of the business need to know that these requirements are applicable to everyone all the time.

- Investing the time and effort in terms of implementing the appropriate documentation, policies, and procedures really is an investment in your business. Not only will the business operate more smoothly with established guidelines and practices, the company will be better protected when problems arise, and this type of framework increases the value of the enterprise and positions it to adopt the professional management approach of a Market Driven Family Business.

- No customer wants to deal with a business that cannot or will not, at a minimum, meet their needs. In fact, the leaders in the marketplace strive to consistently exceed customer expectations, and this can only occur with a competent and professional staff and management group.

TRAPS

- If a member of the business is performing poorly, do not "look the other way". The above average performers in the business are counting on you to resolve the situation.

- Do not consider human resources management to be a "soft" skill area of little importance. The members of the business often represent an organization's most significant investment and resource. Isn't that something worth managing?

Principle Mastery: Recognizing that successful competitors in the marketplace, those operating Market Driven Family Businesses, would not employ your own poorly performing family member puts it in perspective. If the individual is not qualified enough to be an employee in their business, why would you want them in your business?

CHAPTER 5

Perks and Benefits: Engaging Family Members, Tax-Efficiently

The art of living easily as to money is to pitch your scale of living one degree below your means. SIR HENRY TAYLOR

Chuck and Cindy own a cleaning company (C 'n C Cleaning Inc.) which they started up a few years ago. At first, the company provided a way for Cindy to make some extra money after the kids were in school. But in the meantime, the little business has grown so much that Chuck and Cindy now have five full-time employees. Cindy manages and schedules the work and deals with the customers. Chuck still has another full-time job, but he fills in on assignments, picks up supplies and works weekends where necessary.

Chuck and Cindy now have three children: Adam, 18; Kelly, 16; and Todd, 12 years old. Adam and Kelly have also pitched in to work when the business was short staffed. Everyone helps to supervise Todd, who is heavily involved in his hockey and lacrosse schedules, which are both expensive and time consuming, but Todd is excelling.

Like any growing family and business, there are always cash needs. Adam will be going to university in the fall, Cindy needs a new vehicle, and Chuck and Cindy haven't taken a real vacation in years. The company has good cash flow, yet Chuck and Cindy are

reluctant to draw out more cash because, when they do, they see it taxed heavily in their personal hands. Cindy already receives a good salary from the cleaning company and Chuck's salary from his employer put them both in fairly high tax brackets. They are wondering how they can fund all of their cash needs without having to take a really big tax hit.

THE ISSUES

Chuck and Cindy are encountering a number of cash flow issues typical of growing businesses. After consulting with their tax advisor, Brian Thompson, they discovered three main issues they need to address:

- How to plan remuneration and income splitting opportunities with family members
- The potential for funding some of their costs through the corporation
- How to enhance family lifestyle tax-efficiently

Remuneration and income splitting with family members. One of the ways that Chuck and Cindy could lighten their tax burden would be to engage a degree of income splitting within the family. Their children have no external source of their own income, so there is an opportunity to re-channel some of the business earnings to them and save a great deal of tax at the same time.

Individuals are subject to tax, based on a "progressive" tax rate structure. The rates applied to lower levels of income are quite low and then become higher, as an individual's taxable income increases. Therefore, being able to tax income at lower rates in the hands of another family member can achieve significant tax savings through "income splitting" strategies.

Funding certain costs corporately. Chuck and Cindy's tax advisor acknowledged their struggles to fund the twin challenges of a growing family and a growing business. Brian explained that because profits from their business are taxed at much lower rates than income received and taxed to them as individuals, it makes sense to explore whether new strategies could be used to change how the family uses the money earned by the business in order to finance a lot of the family's cash requirements—in short, to use the bigger after-tax corporate dollars first. This sounded good to Chuck and Cindy.

Enhancing family lifestyle tax-efficiently. Chuck and Cindy were previously unaware that business owners can benefit from certain perks or "tax preferences". These perks could form a part of their family compensation from the business, in addition to salary or dividends. The key, explained Brian, is to understand what constitutes a legitimate business outlay and then to take advantage of that opportunity corporately.

THE SOLUTIONS

Chuck and Cindy were actually fascinated as their advisor started to sketch out some of the technical solutions to the dilemma of funding the required remuneration of the family. They also realized that there were some sensitive issues around the payment of family members who worked with other employees of the firm.

Remuneration and Income Splitting with Family Members

First, Brian pointed out that Adam and Kelly often worked in the business—mostly for free! He suggested that a fair and reasonable salary could be paid to them for their efforts. Cindy nodded with agreement. She had often given them an allowance from her own money for helping out, but she never formally paid them from the company as employees.

Their advisor explained that the company could pay the children a salary for services they provided, minus statutory deductions for Canada Pension Plan (CPP)—but only once they turn age 18, as Adam did this year—and income taxes. Because Adam and Kelly are related to the company owners, their employment is not insurable and they would be exempt from Employment Insurance (EI). Brian suggested that he could confirm this treatment with Canada Revenue Agency (CRA). After all, why pay EI premiums, if there is no likelihood of collecting any benefits in the future?

The payment of reasonable salaries to their children will enable the family to fund post-secondary educational requirements as well as enhance their personal lifestyle—all much more tax-efficiently than if the income was earned by mom or dad. That's because Adam and Kelly can use their "personal exemptions" to claim against that income and then pay a relatively low rate of tax on the first $20,000 to $30,000 of income.

For instance, a salary of $20,000 paid to Adam, who will also have $5,000 of eligible tuition fees, results in a very low level of combined federal and provincial taxes. The tax rates will, of course, vary from province to province. In most cases, however, the combined federal and provincial taxes for a single individual with only $20,000 of salary income and $5,000 of tuition will range anywhere from $494 in Alberta to $1,174 in Prince Edward Island. That means that his salary can be used to fund his university tuition (as well as other lifestyle expenses) at a very low tax cost.

"That's a lot less tax than I would pay personally on a $20,000 salary," exclaimed Chuck.

"Precisely," replied their tax advisor.

"Of course, there is another strategy that you can use to 'income split' with your children," the couple learned as Brian continued his 'lesson'. "Dividends—the distribution of after-tax profits in the company—paid to a child 18 years of age or older, can be taxed at very attractive personal rates. It's important that dividends are paid to adult children however, because of what's known as the 'Kiddie Tax'.

"Briefly, the Kiddie Tax works like this: Taxable benefits or dividends from a company paid to a minor child are considered by CRA to be split income. They will be taxed at the top marginal tax rate of the minor. This, in effect, is a disincentive to income split in this fashion, as no advantage is gained. The 'Kiddie Tax' rules do not apply, as long as the dividend is not paid to a minor," he advised.

"So, dividends would work if paid to Adam," interjected Cindy.

"Exactly!" replied Brian. "Kelly will soon be 18 as well, so another tax-efficient income splitting opportunity will arise soon. Not only that, but the first $25,000 to $30,000 of dividend income paid to an individual with no other source of income usually bears little or no personal income tax at all! That's because a tax provision known as the 'dividend tax credit' offsets most, if not all, of the federal and provincial taxes otherwise payable."

"But how can the company pay Adam or Kelly a dividend?" Cindy queried. "Can we just declare a dividend and pay it to them?"

"No, not quite that simple," said Brian. "Adam and Kelly would have to become shareholders in the company or perhaps hold an interest indirectly in the company through a family trust to become entitled to dividends. That's definitely something that can be structured. However, it will take some work to do so and there will be lots of your input required in the process. Because your business is doing so well, I suggest you look at doing so. That's a whole other conversation!"

"Perfect!" exclaimed Chuck. "Let's talk now about how we can pay for Cindy's new car and maybe a trip for the family!"

Funding Costs Corporately

"Good questions, Chuck!"

The tax advisor was enjoying this conversation. He explained that wherever possible and reasonable to do so, it's important to use corporately-earned dollars to fund costs pertaining to the business. For instance, Cindy's new car can be purchased or leased by the company.

"I understand that the company's office is located in your home," he said, "and that Cindy spends a lot of time calling on customers, picking up supplies, and managing the various sites where your employees work."

"That's right," Cindy agreed.

"Would you use your vehicle for business more than 50 percent of the time?"

"Without a doubt," Cindy replied.

"Well, financing the acquisition corporately makes a whole lot of sense, then," Brian explained. "First, your company only pays tax on its profits at the rate of 12%, whereas Cindy's tax rate is easily 40%. Using corporately taxed dollars means that you have roughly 88 cents on the dollar to acquire a vehicle, instead of only 60 cents on the dollar if paid for personally."

"Isn't that a taxable benefit to her?" Chuck chimed in. "I thought that CRA would impose an onerous taxable benefit for the availability of the car for our personal use—isn't it called a standby charge—something like 24% per year on the cost of the vehicle?"

"Yes, that's the general rule," replied the advisor. "However, where a company vehicle is used by the employer in the course of carrying on their employment duties, that 'standby charge' can be reduced, as long as the business use of the vehicle exceeds 50 percent."

"Wow! I'm sure I use my vehicle 80 percent or more for business," said Cindy. "My office is home-based, so every time I go somewhere, it's usually for a business reason!"

Brian explained that the standby charge reduction can be quite substantial if the personal distance driven is a low percentage of the overall distance.

"You might be able to avoid most of this tax entirely. For example, if during the year you drive only 5,000 kilometres on personal reasons, the standby charge otherwise taxable to you can be reduced to 25% of the normal amount." He quickly delivered the actual calculation on the white board: $5,000 / (12 \times 1,667) = 25\%$.

"Those tax savings can be an effective way to finance that new company car!"

"Sounds good," said Chuck. "Now, let's move on to that vacation or maybe some tax deductible travel. What can we do to find some new money for that?"

"Well, personal travel is strictly that," cautioned Brian. "However, many entrepreneurs do travel for business purposes—say a convention or perhaps a business trip to meet with a customer or client. The travel is for business, but it can be a perk as well!"

"Say," Chuck mused, "I've been thinking about attending that trade show in Las Vegas. The show is featuring a lot of new cleaning materials and commercial cleaning equipment. Maybe Cindy and I could go down for a few days and take in the trade show. Would that work?"

"Yes, that should work," replied Brian. "As long as the purpose is clearly to attend the trade show and you keep receipts for your registration, air and hotel, I don't see why you couldn't claim that as a legitimate business expense.

"Also, while we're talking about business trips or conventions, you two should be aware that there are other items which work well if corporately funded. For instance, the life insurance premiums you are paying for personally really should be funded by your company with the company as the owner and beneficiary of the policy."

Chuck admitted, "I've been meaning to ask my financial advisor to do that, but the premiums haven't been that high. But I'm glad you reminded me, because I'm thinking of switching to a permanent whole life policy, and the monthly cash drain is going to be quite a bit."

"Well, now's the time to place that permanent policy within the company. It will be a lot less expensive to finance the non-deductible premiums with corporately taxed dollars, rather than from your own personal pockets. And nothing is lost by doing this. The life insurance proceeds can still be paid out tax-free to your estate through the company's capital dividend account."

"Glad you mentioned that," said Chuck. "Can I ask a couple more questions?"

"Fire away," said their advisor.

"Well, Cindy and I were talking about a few other things…"

"… like a company health plan," said Cindy.

"And maybe a golf membership for me," said Chuck.

That brought the accountant to the third issue.

Enhancing Family Lifestyle Tax-Efficiently

"You have five full-time employees, don't you?" asked the advisor.

"Yes, that's right," said Cindy. "Plus, I receive a salary and Chuck also works in the business—although as you know, he usually doesn't draw a salary. So that's seven, in all."

Brian suggested that the couple consider implementing an employee health services plan, through any of the large insurance companies. The plan will usually provide coverage for prescription drugs, dental, general health services, eyeglasses, as well as long-term disability and also basic life insurance.

The business could pay the monthly premiums and deduct the cost for tax purposes. The plan could provide great coverage for both the family members and the employees.

"A good group benefits plan helps to retain and attract good employees. A word of caution though," their advisor said. "It generally makes sense for all employees to contribute a portion to the plan from their salary so that any future long-term disability benefits can be treated as a tax-free receipt in the event that a claim is made. You should discuss this aspect with your financial advisor in more detail."

"That sounds super," Cindy said. "It will also help us with our personal monthly cash budget, as we've been paying for our own family health and dental plan for years. It will be great to move this cost to our company!"

"So I suppose you want to hear about that golf membership, Chuck," their advisor chuckled.

"You read my mind!" said Chuck.

"Well, strictly speaking, any dues or fees paid in respect of a sporting or club membership are not deductible for tax purposes."

"So, is that a NO?" asked Chuck.

"Well, it depends on the purpose of the membership. If the company pays your dues to a golf membership, it will not be deductible for tax purposes and it may be a taxable benefit to you personally. Unless you can justify that a main purpose of acquiring the membership is to benefit the company and not you personally."

"That's really the reason I want to join," said Chuck. "The club I have my eye on has a lot of members with their own businesses. I figured if I got to know them, and they got to know what we did, I could sell a lot more of our cleaning business. I really want to develop the corporate side of our business and quit my other job in a few years to take this on full time. We could also use the clubhouse for staff functions or perhaps a sales pitch to a new company prospect."

"Well," Brian continued, "you make a good case. But be careful to document the contacts you make and how you use the club for business. This is an area that has some uncertainty to it. If you can show that you have developed new business through the club and have a game plan to use it for that purpose, I think you should be able to avoid a taxable benefit to yourself."

"What about a fitness club membership for me?" asked Cindy.

"For a fitness club, it depends on whether the membership can be considered primarily for the benefit of the employer or the employee. Be aware, however, that even where the membership in a fitness facility is part of an employee-wellness program designed to encourage healthier and better-performing employees, CRA still views the employee as the primary beneficiary of the membership. That means the membership would be considered a taxable employment benefit to you," he said.

IN SUMMARY

This chapter focused on the perks and benefits available to family members as employees and owners of a business. Ways to remunerate and enhance the family lifestyle were examined, and legitimate tax planning opportunities were reviewed.

To be deductible to the company, an outlay or expense must be incurred for the purpose of earning income from the business. Where the outlay or expense potentially confers a benefit on the employee, the amount should still be deductible to the company, providing that it meets the principal business test. Some types of expenditures will result in a taxable benefit being conferred on the employee (such as a company-owned vehicle), while other types of expenditures (a trade show, for instance) primarily benefit the company and would not generally be taxable to the employee, who is attending as a requirement of his employment duties.

Where possible, it is always better to corporately finance the outlay or expenditure, unless the amount is strictly personal, with no business purpose whatsoever.

THINGS YOU NEED TO KNOW

- Corporately finance all business-related expenditures. It is more tax-efficient to do so. Your small business corporation will have roughly 88 cents on each dollar to spend. In contrast, a taxpayer in the top personal tax bracket would have only 54 cents on the dollar to finance business outlays.

- When you or other family-member employees use a vehicle more than 50 percent for business, and drive less than 20,000 personal kilometres per year, it generally makes sense for the company to purchase or lease the vehicle.

- Your lifestyle expenditures can be more tax-efficiently funded when the company pays salaries to family members who work in the business. Tax is minimized by taking advantage of "income splitting".

- Dividends can be paid to family members, but only where they are shareholders in the company, or where they hold a beneficial interest through a family trust. Be aware that the Kiddie Tax rules will apply for dividends paid to a minor.
- Outlays or expenditures made by the company in connection with its business are still deductible to the company, even though a perk or benefit may be conferred on the employee. Make sure the expenditure meets a legitimate business purpose test.

QUESTIONS YOU NEED TO ASK

- Can I pay my family members a salary to income split? What services are they providing or what can they potentially undertake to justify a salary?
- Can I pay my family members dividends from the company's profits? What do I need to do to structure corporate ownership so that "dividend sprinkling" can be achieved?
- Do I have business-related outlays or expenses, which should be paid by the company (i.e. automobile, life insurance, health care premiums)?

THINGS YOU NEED TO DO

- Identify existing expenditures you are making in connection with the business. How are they funded? Personally? Corporately?
- Identify expenditures you intend to make and review business context.
- Review your family and business cash flows with your accountant. Good advice is a prerequisite to good planning.

DECISIONS YOU NEED TO MAKE

- Determine whether you can pay family members a salary or dividend.
- Determine whether certain expenses that are currently paid for personally can instead by paid for by the company.

MASTER YOUR INVESTMENT IN THE FAMILY BUSINESS

Perks and Benefits: Engaging Family Members, Tax-Efficiently

TIPS

- Fund business-related expenditures in the company. The after-tax dollars the company can spend far exceed your after-tax personal dollars!
- Involve family members as employees/owners in the business so that you can "income split" and therefore enhance overall family lifestyle.
- Take advantage of company paid perks (such as travel to a trade show or conference, membership in a sports facility or club, company-sponsored health care plan).

TRAPS

- Be careful that your company does not pay for your family's personal expenses. If there is no business purpose to the expenditure it should be paid for with personal after-tax dollars. Severe penalties can be imposed by CRA for willful neglect in this area.
- Dividends paid to minors will be subject to the "Kiddie Tax". This defeats any income splitting intended, as the highest personal marginal tax rate will apply to all "split-income".
- Be sure to identify expenditures that result in a benefit being conferred on the employee. For instance, while an employee-used vehicle can be purchased and owned by the company, a taxable standby charge should be calculated and added to the employee's T4 slip. Failure to do so can result in adverse tax consequences.

Principle Mastery: Remember that the power of after-tax cash flow is in using your family corporation to fund all business-related expenditures.

CHAPTER 6

Tax-Efficient Bonusing: Maximizing the Small Business Deduction

Share and share alike! DANIEL DEFOE

Ted and Phil own a very successful real estate development corporation. They have been great friends and business partners for years. Each has a 50 percent stake in the company. Real estate has been booming and their company has been successfully riding the tide of increasing demand for new homes. As the market has soared, so have their company profits.

Ted and Phil are just as successful in their personal lives. They each married their high-school sweethearts. Their memories of good times together go back to their double-dating days, high school football games and sock-hops. Each couple has a couple of kids, but the wives and the kids are not involved in their business.

While Ted and Phil are very proud of their company and happy about their good fortune, they both have a single dread every year—having to pay Canada Revenue Agency all those corporate taxes! This year it hurt enough that the partners wondered aloud, "There must be something more we can do about this!"

The issue also caused their first disagreement in years. It was time to get some good advice.

THE ISSUES

For years, Ted and Phil dealt with everything on an even 50/50 split, each taking the same salary. While they still want to run their business that way, Ted and Phil now recognize that they have different personal financial demands. While they wish to continue to deal with their business finances fairly and equitably, they each need to have control over their own 50 percent share of the profits.

Ted had suggested to Phil that they could just bonus out the profits 50/50, and then deal with it personally from there. Phil didn't like the idea of paying all that personal tax and wondered if they might split up the bonuses by paying amounts to their respective spouses and kids. They also both realized that they would have to leave some cash in the company for working capital purposes.

Wisely, Ted and Phil immediately met with their financial advisor, Jim Smith, a certified financial planner, whom they had known for years from high school days. Jim identified three issues facing their business:

- The changing financial needs of each individual family
- The increasing personal tax liabilities of individual partners
- The need to integrate personal and corporate tax planning opportunities

The Changing Financial Needs of Each Individual Family

Jim told the partners that their family and personal financial needs had outgrown their simple and straightforward corporate structure. He indicated that there were other ways they could own and operate the business that could give them more flexibility and control over their respective 50 percent shares, while still dealing with the company profits on an even 50/50 split. Jim suggested they address this with their accountant. He hinted that they might want to consider the use of separate holding companies or perhaps a corporate partnership.

The Increasing Personal Tax Liabilities of Individual Partners

Jim acknowledged Ted and Phil's concern about paying high corporate taxes, but cautioned that the idea of "bonusing out" the profits might simply shift the tax burden from the company to them personally. Phil queried Jim about this, wondering whether they could split the income— that is, divide the bonus between themselves, their wives and their kids. While Jim was not an accountant, he recognized a problem with this strategy. Bonuses are only deductible to the company if paid to a person who actually performs services for the company. Since the wives and kids were not involved in the company, there was no basis for deducting a salary or bonus payable to them. Unfortunately, the partners each would be stuck with the personal tax if they chose to reduce corporate tax using the "bonus route". Of course, Ted and Phil didn't like this option, because they already drew a base $100,000 salary apiece, and any more salary paid to them personally would be taxed at the top marginal tax rate (around 46%).

Jim suggested that they review their corporate/shareholder tax planning with their accountant. He advised that the first $400,000 of profits earned in a company carrying on an active business (such as theirs) is actually taxed at a very low corporate tax rate (anywhere from 11% to 15%, depending on the province). Jim was sure their company was eligible for this annual Small Business Deduction limit of $400,000, which would be increasing to $500,000 next year in their province. The partners could also tap into a similar federal deduction. So it made sense to tax at least that amount of profit in the company. This strategy would also allow them to retain those after-tax profits for working capital purposes.

Ted agreed, but then chuckled and said, "What about the profits over and above that? We're already getting hammered by Revenue Canada!"

"Wow!" Jim exclaimed. "You guys are really doing great, which brings us to the last issue I wanted to raise."

The Need to Integrate Personal and Corporate Tax Planning Opportunities

Jim was a seasoned professional. He knew that company profits in excess of the annual Small Business Deduction ("SBD") limit would be taxed at a higher, but flat corporate tax rate of around 31–33%, depending on the province. Jim pointed out to his clients that, while this rate was considerably higher than the low corporate tax rate, a 31% rate in the company was considerably less than their 46% personal tax rate.

He went on to explain some technical, but important planning concepts. Profits taxed at this higher rate are "notionally" tracked in the company's tax return in an account called the "General Rate Income Pool" (GRIP). Dividends paid out of GRIP can be designated as "eligible dividends". This is important, because on the personal tax return, they receive a preferential tax treatment—better than dividends paid out of corporate surpluses that were subject to the low rate of tax.

Jim suggested that it may not be a bad idea to consider leaving income in excess of the SBD in the company, rather than paying bonuses to them personally. After all, the up-front corporate tax rate of 31% was a lot less than their personal marginal tax rate of 46%, and the opportunity for preferential tax treatment later—perhaps on retirement—might be advantageous to the families.

Ted and Phil had a lot to think about. Their next step was obvious—the partners needed to talk to their accountant about the issues which Jim had raised.

THE SOLUTIONS

Ted and Phil met later that week with their accountant, Bob Black. Bob is a Chartered Accountant who serves their personal and corporate accounting and tax planning requirements well. Bob had been suggesting for several years that the two men take a look at their business structure and do some overall planning. Ted and Phil were now ready to listen and act. Bob suggested a few ideas:

- Incorporating personal holding companies
- Dividend sprinkling with family members
- A corporate partnership

Incorporating Personal Holding Companies

Bob was excited as he discussed one of his favorite topics, personal holding companies.

He explained that Ted and Phil could each incorporate their own personal holding company and transfer their 50 percent shareholding in the operating company to each HOLDCO. Bob suggested that the use of each HOLDCO would enable them to move up the tax-paid corporate surplus from the operating company to each HOLDCO by way of a tax-free inter-corporate dividend. Profits and tax would still be earned and paid at the OPCO level, but the use of the two HOLDCOs would allow the partners to "clean out" the corporate profits each year and then have the flexibility to deal with the surplus individually at the HOLDCO level.

There was more good news. Bob suggested that they could make their wives and kids shareholders at the HOLDCO level and implement a plan to do some "dividend sprinkling" within the families.

Dividend Sprinkling with Family Members

As one might imagine, Ted jumped on the idea of family income splitting and immediately asked Bob about paying salaries or bonuses to family members from the HOLDCO level. Unfortunately this would not be possible.

"I'm afraid not, Ted. There actually won't be any taxable income at the HOLDCO level as the dividends move up tax-free to the HOLDCOs."

"Why is that?" asked Ted.

Bob explained, "That's because when one corporation pays a dividend to another connected corporation, the dividend income is not subject to tax in the recipient corporation. In effect, corporate surplus is simply being moved from one company to another. Your HOLDCO is connected with the OPCO because it would own more than 10 percent of the voting shares of the OPCO. The dividend would therefore not create any taxable income in your HOLDCO, and any deduction for a salary or bonus paid to your family members would be wasted within the HOLDCO."

"So what if we have the OPCO pay up a management fee or something to each HOLDCO?" asked Phil. "That way, there'll be a deduction in OPCO and income in each HOLDCO. Couldn't we pay salaries to the wives and kids and flow the income through that way?"

"Whoa!" cautioned Bob. "Inter-company management fees can be a problem. CRA could take an unfavourable view of inter-company fees that are nothing more than a recharacterization of your salaries from OPCO. The deduction of the management fee to OPCO could also be denied, if there is no service or contract to justify the payment, and similarly no individual performing services at the HOLDCO level to OPCO. The HOLDCOs work best for inter-company dividends, not inter-company management fees."

However, Bob drew out another potential solution.

A Corporate Partnership

A corporate partnership can provide the solution to many of the obstacles Ted and Phil had identified with their financial advisor. Bob explained to the partners how this structure could help.

A corporate partnership addresses the issue of meeting family financial needs by giving each partner the ability to deal with his share of the profits in the way he thinks will benefit his own family best. The split would still be fair and equitable—50/50 all the way.

Second, the use of a corporate partnership makes it easier to structure a salary or bonus to family members, as family members might provide a service to each company in the form of bookkeeping, record-keeping, or marketing assistance. The salaries must be reasonable, but there were plenty of good case law precedents to support reasonable salaries paid to family members.

Third, the business profits would now be taxed at each corporate partner level and not within the partnership. Each family could make its own decisions to maximize the use of its company's annual SBD limit, pay tax on general rate income, and then be able to pay out "eligible dividends" to family members. This effectively creates a basis to do some income splitting or "dividend sprinkling", thereby reducing the family's overall tax burden.

Here's how Bob would help the partners make it work:

Ted and Phil's OPCO could transfer or roll all of their operating assets and business to a partnership comprised of two new companies. The rollover or transfer could be achieved on a tax-deferred basis. Each new corporate partner could be organized to include other family members as shareholders. Their existing OPCO would also take back a partnership interest, but the value could be fixed with an entitlement to a fixed percentage of the profits in the new venture.

Bob explained that profits in the new partnership would be taxable to each corporate partner on a 50/50 basis, and that the income would be treated as active business income subject to the SBD limit in each corporate partner. The companies would have to share the annual SBD limit, but that was something they were sharing now anyway. Bob suggested that they could then "individualize" tax plans for each family by having Ted and Phil employed at the corporate partner level. Profits would still flow up on a 50/50 basis, but each partner could make individual decisions about bonuses, salaries to family members (provided they provided some service to the HOLDCO), dividend sprinkling to each family member, and the level of income they wished to retain and tax within each corporation.

Over time, the old OPCO could be paid out its interest in the partnership and then eventually liquidated or wound up. Bob explained that this restructuring was called a "partnership freeze". It froze the old OPCO's interest in the business, and restructured it as a partnership so that each family's HOLDCO might participate equally, but also tailor their tax planning separately.

Ted and Phil took this all in, then said to Bob, "When do we start?"

IN SUMMARY

This chapter focused on the issues pertaining to the use of bonuses or other similar remuneration to business owners, in contrast to retaining profits within the company and having those profits taxed corporately.

Decisions around the level and type of remuneration payable to the business owner depend on a number of factors, including:

- The owner's need for personal cash,
- The marginal tax rate of the owner,
- The corporate income level (income eligible for the SBD versus income included as GRIP).

To be deductible by the company, a payment of a bonus or salary must be reasonable in the circumstances, and the payee must have performed some level of service that would justify or indicate that the bonus was paid in connection with and for the purpose of earning income.

In contrast, there is no such test required for the payment of a dividend to a family member, other than the requirement that the person be a shareholder of the corporation.

Where there are arm's length shareholders or different family interests in the company, structuring remuneration purely through a "bonus route" can be quite inflexible. Corporate structure therefore plays an important role in the overall remuneration strategies and options for the family shareholders.

THINGS YOU NEED TO KNOW

- Your corporation (if it carries on an active business) has an annual Small Business Deduction (SBD) limit, which enables the first $400,000 of profits to be taxed at very low rates. The federal government is moving to a $500,000 SBD limit commencing in 2009.

- Profits in excess of the SBD allocated to your company for the year are taxed at a higher corporate rate, but they are included in GRIP—and that's a good thing because "eligible dividends", which are taxed at advantageous tax rates personally, can be paid out of GRIP.

- Bonuses or remuneration to family members must be based on services or work which they reasonably performed for the company. The payment of unreasonable remuneration is not deductible by the company.

- Corporate structure plays an integral role in structuring effective remuneration and income splitting strategies with owners and their families.

QUESTIONS YOU NEED TO ASK

- Does my company qualify for the annual SBD?
- How do I maximize the bonus/corporate income model for my family situation?
- Is my corporate structure optimizing my remuneration and income splitting opportunities?
- Can I reasonably pay and deduct salaries or other remuneration to family members?

THINGS YOU NEED TO DO

- Review corporate structure with your business partners and financial advisors, in context of your individual and family needs for remuneration.

- Assess and review owner/company remuneration planning annually with your accountant to establish optimal salary/dividend plan.

- Review ways of involving family members in the company in order to provide a reasonable basis for payment of salaries (i.e. income splitting).

DECISIONS YOU NEED TO MAKE

- Decide on a corporate structure that best fits the owners' needs and cash flow requirements.

- Determine if involving family members in the structure is feasible.

MASTER YOUR INVESTMENT IN THE FAMILY BUSINESS

Tax-Efficient Bonusing: Maximizing the Small Business Deduction

TIPS

- Retain and pay tax on income within the company wherever possible, if there is not a personal need for cash. Corporate tax is a great deal less than paying tax at top personal marginal rates.
- When additional cash is required to fund personal or family needs, look at alternatives to a bonus to the owners. For instance, where possible consider:
  - Bonuses or salaries to other family members (for services performed).
  - Dividends to other family members (as shareholders). This is effective "dividend sprinkling".
- Review remuneration strategies at least annually with your accountant.

TRAPS

- Be careful about paying salaries or bonuses to family members where you cannot justify that any reasonable service was provided. Such payments can be denied as a deduction to the company, but still taxed to the payee. Double tax can result!
- Be aware that your corporate structure might trap you, your business partner and your families into making ineffective decisions about your remuneration strategies.
- Be very careful about structuring inter-company management fees. This area should be reviewed in detail by your tax accountant and tax lawyer. It can be fraught with pitfalls.

Principle Mastery: Maximize the use of the annual SBD limit. Corporate tax rates are low. You can build wealth within the corporate model.

CHAPTER 7

Incorporating
Non-Family Members

Sister Act JOSEPH HOWARD

Twin sisters Natalie and Jessica are architects. They own and manage an architectural firm that works on both residential and commercial projects. They have been in business for five years. With the recent economic conditions, they have found themselves doing fewer large commercial projects, but business has picked up in the home expansion and renovation area, which has meant more work for Jessica and her three staff members. Natalie and her team, who work on the commercial side of the business, have had less work to do.

Jessica, backlogged with projects and without enough staff members who have senior level experience, would like to hire an architect with work experience to speed up the work flow. Natalie has suggested that since this new role would be senior to the rest of the staff that it should be held by a family member. Their niece, Emily, is currently studying interior design and works part-time in the business. Emily will graduate in just over a year, and although she has been working mostly on the commercial side of the business, Natalie believes that she would be a good candidate to help Jessica with her increased workload.

Jessica is not convinced. Although promoting Emily could provide a quick solution, she is concerned about Emily's lack of work experience and architectural skills and does not believe that she would be senior enough to competently take on the position at this point. But, Jessica wonders, would hiring an external person be "de-motivating" to Emily, who with the proper training and experience could be a good candidate for the position in a few years? On the other hand, if she brought in someone from the outside who is not a family member, she wonders what type of compensation structure would be expected and whether an ownership position in the business would be required.

THE ISSUES

Jessica and Natalie need to quickly resolve their work backlog in order to meet the needs and expectations of their clients. Given the specialized nature of their business, the work must be done properly and is best performed by those with specialized education, experience, and professional designations. Emily may possess some of the necessary requirements, but likely not all of them, and is a few years away from even being a strong candidate to hold the position.

It may seem obvious that Jessica and Natalie need to look to a qualified non-family member to hold the position they plan to create, but in many family businesses, the temptation can be to give the position to a family member whose qualifications are "close enough" to achieve a quick solution and maintain family harmony. This can represent a significant mistake, regardless of the type of business.

What happens when a family business grows to a point where more specialized resources are required? Unless the family business leader has been setting expectations and gearing family members towards obtaining the necessary education and experience to hold key positions, as described earlier in this book, the business may have to look to other options, including hiring qualified non-family members to hold these important roles.

However, bringing on non-family members to hold key positions in the business can backfire, unless they are properly integrated into the business. An environment must exist where non-family members feel welcome, fairly treated, and that the opportunity exists for them to advance to more senior positions, as opposed to watching, day after day, priority being given to family members, whether they possess the necessary qualifications or not. These talented individuals will leave the business to pursue other opportunities, if this is the case, thereby limiting the growth and potential of the business, to the detriment of the family.

Consider the following:

- In the case of family business leaders who hold specialized training, like Jessica and Natalie, qualified non-family members represent a useful resource that can take on some of the excess workload in key areas. **This allows the business to do more, immediately.**

- In the case of family business leaders who do not have specialized training, it is important to bring on non-family members who have specialized expertise in order to expand the technical ability and offerings of the business. **This allows the business to do new things today and improve its competitive position in the market-place for desired results tomorrow.**

  However, if not managed properly, complications can arise:

  - Depending on the personality and attributes of the family business leader, they may begin to feel overshadowed or threatened by an employee who has more knowledge than they do.

  - Depending on the particular situation, the non-family member employee may feel isolated in a business where there are no senior people that they can "learn from", due to the lack of specialized knowledge at the top of the organization.

  - A non-family member employee may also feel uncomfortable if the rationale for their joining the business has not been explained to other family members, and they may experience resentment, given that there is not a family member in the position.

- Family members who do not have the skills and experience to hold the particular position may also be dissatisfied, if the rationale for hiring a qualified non-family member was not properly explained or implemented. If family members do not have specialized expertise, they may not appreciate the specific job requirements and may hold the view that they themselves are sufficiently qualified to hold the position; that is, "they don't know what they don't know". This type of situation can result in everything from resentment of the non-family member, to undermining, and even worse behavior. **This type of situation has the potential to damage the business.**

Family business leaders need to have a strategy and approach for bringing qualified non-family members into the business. This is particularly important in the case of Market Driven Family Businesses, as they seek to successfully compete in the marketplace, which requires having an appropriately qualified individual in every position, family member or otherwise. How can such a strategy be developed and implemented?

THE SOLUTIONS

Creating an environment where qualified non-family members can make a meaningful contribution to the business, thereby increasing the wealth of the family, considers the needs of the organization, as well as the personal and professional needs of the non-family member (i.e., compensation, decision-making ability, professional development, a sense of belonging, etc.). If these needs are met, the opportunity to bring the best qualified resources into the business is created, thereby raising the likelihood of the business successfully competing in the marketplace and generating wealth for the family.

Qualified non-family members can supplement the ability of the family business leader(s), in terms of picking up some of the workload or providing skills and expertise that are not currently held by the business. This, in turn, creates the opportunity to train and develop others.

Let's consider some of the key components that must be addressed to successfully integrate qualified non-family members into the business, especially at a senior level.

Reinforce the Need for Specialized Skills and Experience

As discussed in Chapter 3, a Market Driven Family Business needs specific skills and experience to be successful. If family members are taught to focus on what is best for the business as the most appropriate approach for generating wealth for the family, as opposed to focusing on family member situations, this will be obvious to them.

Bringing on a qualified non-family member is one approach that can be used to bring specialized expertise to a family business. Another approach is to utilize a non-family member as an interim resource, as perhaps in the case of Emily, where a potential qualified family member is not quite ready to take on the position. This type of staged approach could meet the needs of a non-family member who is looking for a senior level engagement for a finite period of time, perhaps just prior to retirement, and can also provide a mentorship opportunity for the newly qualified family member to transition into the job. This can also represent an attractive stepping stone to qualified individuals looking to build their careers.

The key is to set expectations for family members and remind them to focus on the needs of the business. *Remember, what is important is that the business has the right expertise to be successful, regardless of the source.*

Remind Family Members of Their Choice

Once family members have been engaged in a communication process that sets consistent expectations for the requirements and qualifications to join the business, they should be empowered to make a decision as to whether they wish to be actively or passively involved in the business. If they choose to be actively involved, this must be contingent upon their achievement of the necessary qualifications to perform the particular job. *They must make a deliberate choice, qualify, and make a formal commitment. Only then can they join 'the club.'*

This is very important and it is a scenario that must be remembered when the time comes for family succession planning. Those who had to qualify, commit, and then actively participate in building the business need to be acknowledged accordingly throughout the process.

In the event that the business requires specialized expertise, family members should realize that it is within their "control" to pursue the necessary education and/or training to be a candidate for a position in the business. They should also recognize that it is up to the family business leader to identify the individual that is best suited for the position, family member or otherwise, with the guiding objective being *the best interest of the business.* When this approach is taken, family members should realize that a qualified non-family member is not being "imposed" on them; rather, the situation should be viewed as a solution for the ongoing health of the business, with family members having a clear choice as to whether they wish to take the steps to be the right candidate for the position or not.

Compensate Positions Based on Their Relative Worth to the Business

Sometimes family businesses focus on maximizing the ownership position and compensation of family members regardless of their ability to add value to the business, with the sole criteria being family member status. This approach is not appropriate for a Market Driven Family Business.

If a family business requires specialized expertise that is not currently held by family members, an attractive employment opportunity, including a competitive compensation package, must be provided. Some in the family may consider this approach to be little more than diverting funds away from the family; however, this view misses the real opportunity.

The family business leader who is able to attract a highly skilled candidate, at the appropriate level of compensation, is really making an investment in building the business and future wealth for the family. The business must have the required policies, procedures, and infrastructure to take on the right resources and hire skilled professionals to help the company operate more independently of the founder and the family, which is an important factor in the transitioning of the business from one stage of development and growth to another.

Well-qualified candidates not only represent the opportunity for enhanced growth of the enterprise, through high achievement and strong job performance, they also can transfer skills and knowledge to others in the business. Even in the case where the family business leader has specific technical skills, such as Jessica and Natalie, a younger professional can bring new and current approaches to the business, which can benefit all members of the business, including the family business leaders. These individuals can also represent a future succession opportunity, in the absence of qualified family members that could take over the business.

In most cases, compensation should include a base salary and performance component (i.e., bonus, profit sharing, etc.), as well as an employee benefits plan (i.e., health, dental, insurance, etc.). Sales-based positions typically include a significant commission component based on sales activity. In order to attract quality candidates, family business leaders should first spend time developing their organizational chart and its link to the business performance plan.

Then, they should seek out information in terms of appropriate compensation levels for a particular position as a starting point for developing a compensation package. This information is usually readily available, particularly by way of industry salary surveys and interaction with human resource professionals.

A salary range can then be developed for the position, which provides the opportunity for advancement within the position, as well as the flexibility to adjust the salary level depending on the qualifications of a particular candidate.

Performance-based compensation, such as bonuses and profit sharing, is an important component for attracting high quality candidates. Achievement-oriented individuals typically enjoy having performance targets and the opportunity to be compensated for achieving them. This is a good approach for the business as well, as compensation is paid only if and when the pre-determined performance targets are met.

Although the structure of performance targets can take various forms, a good approach is to combine individual targets for the particular position (i.e., satisfactory performance of all job tasks, meeting professional development requirements, satisfactory working relationships with others, etc.) with targets that relate to performance of the business (i.e., sales, profitability, successful launch of new products and services, etc.). This blended approach reduces the likelihood of performance solely in the best interest of the individual, and perhaps at the expense of the business, and requires a component of teamwork to make the business successful as well.

Determine if Ownership is an Issue

In many family businesses, there is an attitude that ownership of the business should be limited solely to family members. In some Lifestyle Family Businesses or an extremely successful Market Driven Family Business that is comprised of many well-qualified family members, this may be appropriate. However, there are many family businesses whose performance and circumstances fall between these two extremes. These companies should consider the implications of making ownership opportunities available to those from outside of the family.

Ownership could be structured in a variety of ways, including the opportunity to acquire various share classes within the business (i.e., voting and non-voting, for example), stock options, phantom stock options (i.e., no shares are issued, but compensation is based on the actual performance of the company's stock), and agreements to transfer shares at some future point in time. Given that structuring and implementing such types of transactions and programs involves considerable effort, thought, and advisory fees for the development and maintenance of the arrangement, ownership programs should not be pursued unless they are meaningful to the recipient. It is well worth the effort for the family business leader to determine the meaningfulness of this type of structure through direct discussion with potential candidates, as opposed to assuming whether it is relevant or not, as the wrong assumption can be a costly mistake either way.

For key employees who are non-family members, especially at a senior level and where a succession opportunity may exist, ownership can create the opportunity for significant motivation for the employee and wealth generation for the business, and ultimately the family. Although the structure and specific requirements will vary with the individual, if a family business leader is serious about growing the business to a new level, the issue of ownership is something that is certainly worth exploring, and may provide more benefits to the business, in comparison to the "cost" of what is given up. Remember, the goal is to motivate and retain the qualified non-family member, and this type of approach can be the difference between a satisfied employee, as opposed to one who walks out the door, perhaps to join your competitor.

Avoid Employee "Classes" in the Businesses

Some family businesses operate in such a way that there are special, albeit, unwritten rules for family members in the business, as compared to non-family members. This type of "class" structure, where the sole defining factor is whether or not an individual is a family member, can be destructive for a business, particularly one that seeks to operate on the level of a Market Driven Family Business.

Qualified non-family members, particularly those who hold key positions in the business, will not be enamored with situations where there is not a level playing field, in terms of what good performance can accomplish. Situations where compensation is determined based on the value of the job to the organization for non-family members, whereas family members actively involved in the business are compensated arbitrarily, and perhaps, at a premium, solely for being family members will likely have the impact of driving out qualified non-family members.

Family members should be compensated fairly based on the value of the job that they perform, with any ownership or family-related compensation components being addressed separately. This type of approach creates a level playing field, for family and non-family members, in terms of compensation and the value they are expected to bring to the organization. The same approach can be taken for other related areas, such as performance feedback, opportunities for advancement, and input in terms of decision making.

Although these may seem like small things, utilizing this approach can provide the difference between non-family members feeling that they have a real opportunity to contribute to the business, being fairly compensated based on their performance, and having access to opportunities for advancement, as opposed to facing a brick wall entitled "family members only".

The only way to achieve this is through the appropriate formality: everyone needs to sign employment contracts, undergo job interviews and performance reviews, and share in team rewards. This requires transparent human resource policies backed by legal agreements and company-wide adherence to policies and procedures.

Encourage Professional Development and Integration

Professional development, training programs, and access to skill-enhancing opportunities are critical in fostering a learning environment in the business. Professional integration with others in a particular profession or discipline can be particularly important in situations where a qualified non-family member is brought into a business to provide a specific type of expertise.

In this type of situation, the family business leader and other members of the organization do not have the type of expertise that they are hiring (i.e., engineering, accounting, etc.). Qualified non-family members that join this type of family business hold an important role, as they may provide the specialized knowledge and expertise to take the business to a new level. The issue is that these type of professionals can feel isolated in this type of organization, as they do not have access to anyone at a senior or peer level that can provide mentorship and support. These individuals may therefore leave the business to pursue opportunities where they can have daily access to others that share their expertise.

By encouraging regular professional development and interaction with a peer group or professional association outside of the business, family business leaders can provide the exposure that well-qualified non-family members require in order to feel connected to their profession. Many of the fees for these programs are tax deductible for the business, and bring a far greater benefit to the business than the actual cost of the program. This approach can keep qualified non-family members motivated and performing well, transferring new knowledge to the business, and minimize the likelihood of these individuals leaving the business for a less isolating environment.

Address Inappropriate Behavior

Despite the best intentions and communication efforts of a family business leader, some family members may still feel compelled to express their dissatisfaction with non-family members holding key positions within the family business. This is unacceptable, and must be addressed by the family business leader immediately in order to avoid damage to the business and the possible loss of qualified individuals.

The steps that are taken to correct the inappropriate behavior will vary with the situation; however, whatever the approach, it must be effective in resolving the matter. If a family business leader is at a loss as to how to deal with the problem, consulting a human resources professional can be helpful in terms of identifying approaches to resolve the situation.

Family members must understand that the best interest of the business must be the focus, and anything less than that comes at the expense of the business and the family as a whole. Non-family members must make the same commitment to contribute respectfully to the growth of the enterprise as a whole.

IN SUMMARY

Qualified individuals are a critical resource for any business. It is important to create an environment within the business for talented individuals to feel welcome and an important part of the business, as opposed to feeling like an outsider.

Compensation that is consistent with the value of the position, the potential for an ownership position, consistent treatment of family and non-family members, and access to professional development and peer groups outside of the business can help all qualified members of the business feel comfortable and that the business is treating them fairly. The family business leader should also recognize that opportunities for advancement within the business should be based on merit. All members of the business must know how to advance in a transparent environment.

In particular, family members should be taught the importance of the skills and experience that qualified non-family members bring, and any inappropriate behavior and interference from family members should be corrected immediately by the family business leader. Making the family business a welcome place for qualified non-family members is in the best interest of the business, as it can provide the opportunity for enhanced performance, profitability, and even a long-term succession plan in the absence of qualified family members.

THINGS YOU NEED TO KNOW

- Qualified non-family members represent a powerful opportunity to improve the performance of your business and transfer useful skills and expertise, particularly in terms of businesses that do not possess a lot of professional or technical knowledge.
- Qualified non-family members can represent a succession opportunity in the absence of qualified family members, and should be compensated and treated in a manner that preserves this opportunity.
- Qualified non-family members considering joining a family business, for the most part, want to be treated fairly, in terms of compensation, input, and advancement opportunity. Failing to do so can result in these talented individuals leaving the business to pursue other opportunities, perhaps with your competitors.

QUESTIONS YOU NEED TO ASK

- Does the business require expertise and/or additional help that cannot be provided by family members?
- For qualified non-family members currently working in the business, are they being treated fairly, in terms of compensation, input, and opportunities for advancement?
- Does your business have employee "classes", in terms of family and non-family members?
- Does your business encourage professional development and interaction, particularly those who hold professional designations and/or key positions in the business?
- Are family members who are active in the business treating non-family members appropriately, and vice versa, or are there behavioral issues that require immediate resolution?
- Have any qualified non-family members left the business? If so, why?
- Have any qualified family members left the business? If so, why?
- Do you currently have an appropriate business succession plan, or should you be considering the potential for qualified non-family members to fulfill this role?

THINGS YOU NEED TO DO

- Identify areas of the business where specific assistance and/or expertise is required. Set priorities in terms of which position(s) should be filled first, and incorporate this into the business' annual operating plan.

- Obtain competitive compensation information for similar positions, by way of salary survey or assistance from a human resources professional.

- Review your business in terms of compensation, input, advancement, and other areas for family and non-family members to ensure that inequity does not exist between the two groups. Resolve any differences to eliminate an employee class structure.

- Consider the opportunity for staging particular positions in the business, where junior or inexperienced family members are not currently ready to hold a position. A qualified non-family member can hold the position for a period of time, transfer knowledge to the business, and act as a mentor to transition a family member into the position at some future point in time.

- Consider the status of your succession plan and determine if qualified non-family members are required to develop a suitable plan.

DECISIONS YOU NEED TO MAKE

- Determine how skill and workload assistance requirements of the business will be handled, now and in the future. Are there qualified family members, or is looking outside the family a better solution?

- If you are currently looking to bring on a qualified non-family member, determine and implement the appropriate strategy for doing so.

MASTER YOUR INVESTMENT IN THE FAMILY BUSINESS
Incorporating Non-Family Members

TIPS

- Reconfirm your commitment to operate as a Market Driven Family Business and make the best decision for the business, in terms of the most appropriate individual to hold key positions, family member or otherwise.

- Being "the smartest person in the business" can be extremely lonely and not sustainable for professionals who seek daily interaction with others in their profession. Encouraging professional development and interaction outside of the organization can be an important strategy in retaining qualified non-family members with specialized skills in a family business where the leaders possess limited professional expertise.

- Do not underestimate the value that a qualified non-family member can bring to your business, including new and specialized knowledge, technical skills, a personal network, professionalism, and a high degree of motivation. These individuals provide the opportunity to energize your business and encourage others to perform better and pursue advanced training and education.

- Develop transparent policies and procedures as the framework for operating the business in a competitive market environment. Don't let the internal obstacles keep you from being of service to your customers or those who wish to be your customers in the future.

TRAPS

- Family business leaders who feel threatened by talented non-family members need an attitude adjustment. These individuals have the potential to add significant value to your business, so create an environment where they are motivated to perform at their best and celebrate their accomplishments!

Principle Mastery: When you look around your business and see individuals for the job they do, the value they bring to the business, and the potential they hold, as opposed to seeing family and non-family members, you have achieved an organization without employee classes where all members of the business can work as a team to their best potential.

CHAPTER 8

The Estate Freeze–
When is it Time?

Put not your trust in money, but put your money in trust.
OLIVER WENDELL HOLMES

Bill and Margaret own a great company. Bill is 62 and Margaret is 59. They have three children, Jan, Ryan and Willy (Bill Jr.). Jan and Ryan are real go-getters and after graduation from university, they got involved in the family business. Jan's Bachelor of Commerce in marketing is proving to be a real asset to the business. She works directly with the VP in marketing. Ryan is an engineer and is con- tributing greatly to the company's production line and "just-in- time" delivery systems. Willy, the baby of the family, is still figuring out what he wants to do. He likes the arts and he likes fast cars! Willy is also a lot of fun at a party!

Bill and Margaret love all three kids dearly. They want to be fair to all three in whatever they do with the business and they also want to transition the business to them. They have a good feeling about Jan and Ryan in the business. They aren't shareholders now, but they show the signs of leadership and entrepreneurial spirit. They don't know where Willy is headed yet.

Bill is thinking of giving Jan and Ryan some shares in the business now, as a perk or bonus for doing so well. Margaret is concerned that might not be fair to Willy and she is also worried how that might affect Willy's dealings with his siblings.

Bill also thinks that there are a couple of key people in the business who should get some shares. They were there at the beginning and were instrumental in making the company what it is today. Bill is worried they might harbour some resentment if they don't get a chance at ownership. It might not sit well with them if his kids just walked in as owners.

Bill and Margaret often talked about these matters—usually with no clear-cut direction emerging. There were so many things to consider, and life with adult children and a growing business was not about to get simpler! Bill and Margaret needed help with ongoing decision making to keep harmony in both these important aspects of their lives.

THE ISSUES

For Bill and Margaret, several important issues were evolving with their growing business, which they decided wisely to discuss with their trusted family financial advisor, Sandra Connolly. She listened carefully to Bill and Margaret explain their family and business dynamic, taking careful notes. After a brief pause to compose her thoughts, Sandra sat back and identified the key issues for these clients:

- Business succession planning
- Tax issues to consider
- Fairness when children are introduced as owners
- Including non-family members in the plan
- Planning and valuation for business succession

Business succession planning. There truly is a business succession issue at hand and the time to deal with it is now. While Bill and Margaret have pondered this matter for years, it is clear that the time to act has arrived. A plan is necessary and it will take time to develop one.

Tax issues to consider. There are certainly tax and valuation issues interconnected with any effective estate or business succession plan. When Sandra had listened to Bill's idea of simply gifting a few shares to his children now, she pointed out that a gift of shares would trigger an unexpected tax consequence. Any transfer or gift of shares represents a disposition for tax purposes and a resulting capital gain. Without proper planning, they would be facing a tax bill on the capital gain.

Fairness when children are introduced as owners. Sandra acknowledged Margaret's concerns over the fairness or appearance of fairness in introducing some family members as owners, and pointed out that introducing children directly as shareholders can create other potential problems in the future. For instance, there could be possible claims from relationships they may enter into, or perhaps the risk that those shares could be exposed to their creditors.

Including non-family members in the plan. The advisor noted that there are pros and cons in bringing in non-family members as shareholders. The prospect of ownership to a key employee can be a powerful and rewarding incentive. However, such persons would be minority shareholders with minority-shareholder rights. There could be times in the future when the family might be "handcuffed" from moving in a particular direction, because of minority-shareholder interests. Also dealing with employee share turnover, valuation and liquidation of their shares could become a complicating factor.

Planning and valuation for business succession. Finally, Sandra asked Bill and Margaret what they wanted to see in the way of cash from the value of the company once they set up a transition and succession plan.

While she knew that Bill and Margaret had a fair amount of non-registered investments built up in their portfolio, she wondered whether they were content to give their children the company or whether they should somehow pay for the shares. This issue opened up a new dialogue. Bill thought his kids should pay for the shares or somehow earn them. Margaret wasn't against that idea, but she wondered how they would possibly come up with the money to do that. Jan and Ryan were each paid a good salary from the company, but she knew they didn't have the kind of funds necessary to buy out their shares. Will Jr. wasn't working.

The two key employees they had in mind probably didn't have that kind of cash either.

THE SOLUTIONS

Bill and Margaret's company generated good cash flow—and that certainly was a prerequisite for many of the plans they hoped to put into place for their future. Maybe the kids and the employees could be paid bonuses which they could use to buy out their shares. Bill liked the idea of getting some cash for his shares; he had his eye on a condo in Palm Springs! However, he didn't want to make it too tough for his kids to come up with the money either.

Surely there was some way to make this work. Their financial advisor assured them that, in fact, there were two potential solutions:

- Sell the shares
- Use an estate freeze

Sell the Shares

One way to accomplish this would be for Bill and Margaret to sell their shares to their children and a few key employees. It would be necessary to place a fair value on the shares of the company. They would probably need a business valuator to do so. Of course, their children and key employees would have to be agreeable to the price and terms of sale. A proper valuation would be a must, as the majority of the transfer would occur to non-arm's length persons (their children) and Canada Revenue Agency would be interested to know that no "undue benefit" or "gift" occurred as a result of the sale or transfer.

This transaction would result in a disposition of Bill and Margaret's shares in the company, and a resulting capital gain to each of them. Sandra indicated that they probably would qualify for the $750,000 Lifetime Capital Gains Exemption (LCGE), but that they should confirm this tax treatment with their accountant.

The advisor further suggested that Bill and Margaret could structure the sale so that the purchasers made an initial cash down payment, while the vendors (Bill and Margaret) took back a note for the balance of the share price. This strategy is termed a "vendor take-back". One advantage of this strategy is that it would enable Bill and Margaret to spread out any tax consequences of the sale over a number of years while also providing the purchasers with a term of several years to come up with the necessary cash.

However, Sandra also correctly pointed out a few drawbacks in going with a direct sale of shares.

- **Loss of control.** A sale of shares effectively creates an immediate loss of control in the company for Bill and Margaret. They no longer would own shares and they would no longer have a say in how the company was run. They would have rights set out in the Share Purchase Agreement in the event the purchasers defaulted on payment, but those rights would not give them any day-to-day control over the company anymore, nor any voting rights on key strategic decisions by the company shareholders. Bill didn't much like the idea of completely giving up control.

- **Immediate tax consequences.** A sale of shares triggers tax consequences to the vendors. Bill and Margaret may be able to each use their $750,000 LCGE, but if the capital gain exceeds $1.5 million, they will end up paying tax on the excess.

  "Ouch! That's a problem," said Bill. "I think our company is worth well in excess of 1.5 million!"

- **After-tax dollars must finance the purchase.** The purchasers will be obligated to finance the share acquisition with after-tax dollars. Even if the company pays them a bonus or dividend, they will have to pay personal tax on that income, and then use the after-tax funds to finance the acquisition. The same holds true if their children go out and borrow funds to make the acquisition. While the interest on the debt may be tax-deductible, the principal portion of the debt is not, and it must be repaid with after-tax dollars.

- **Careful documentation is required for inter-family transactions.** A non-arm's length sale of shares also poses other tax complexities. Where a related vendor (i.e. father, mother) claims the $750,000 LCGE, certain restrictions are imposed on the non-arm's length purchaser in respect of a subsequent disposition of the shares by them. For instance, they would be unable to transfer their shares to a holding company in the same manner and fashion as someone who dealt at arm's length with their parents, without suffering adverse tax consequences. Due care and consideration would have to be observed to track the family history of such transactions.

- **The sales transaction is irreversible.** A sale of shares to a particular person can also be somewhat irreversible. What if a particular employee becomes problematic and it is no longer desirable for that individual to also be a shareholder? An employee share-ownership agreement might deal with such issues but it nonetheless creates complexities. What if Willy's ownership in the company becomes a source of conflict with his siblings? It may be possible for his brother and sister to buy out his interest—perhaps at the cost of family harmony.

Bill and Margaret were frowning and starting to worry that it was going to be too difficult to make this all happen. Their financial advisor sensed their concerns and said reassuringly, "There is a better solution!"

Use an Estate Freeze

In a situation like the one Bill and Margaret face, there are benefits to using an estate freeze over a direct sale of shares as a solution. You may recall from a previous chapter that an estate freeze is a method by which Bill and Margaret would "swap" or exchange their common shares for a fixed value of preference or "freeze" shares. The exchange can be undertaken on a tax-deferred basis. In effect, the shares are deemed to be disposed of for proceeds equal to their cost which results in no capital gains or loss for tax purposes.

"That sounds a lot better," said Bill.

Then, once all of the existing share value is transferred or "frozen" into these new preference shares, the company can issue new common growth shares to any number of new shareholders.

"Like our children," exclaimed Margaret.

"Exactly," said Sandra. "Those shares can be issued and paid for with nominal consideration, such as $1.00 per share. All of the future growth and value of the company will now accrue to the benefit of the new common shareholders."

"But how does that leave Margaret and I in terms of control over the company?" asked Bill.

"Good question", replied the advisor. "You, in effect exchanged your existing shares for fixed value preference shares. Instead of the purchasers owing you money, as is the case of a sale, your company owes you that value, locked into the redemption amount of such freeze shares. Over time, your company can redeem these shares and pay you out for the full value of your company today.

"Better still," continued Sandra, "you and Margaret can retain complete voting control over the company by virtue of the freeze shares you hold. Until the last share is redeemed and you are fully paid out, you and Margaret can retain such control."

Therefore, for this situation in particular, an estate freeze can then be used to achieve specific goals:

- Unlike a sale, there is no loss of control over the corporation.
- The transfer of the business occurs with corporately taxed dollars. There is no requirement for their children to borrow funds personally or to use highly taxed personal funds to finance the acquisition. Instead, Bill and Margaret would be paid over time from the existing cash flow of their company. In effect, the future profits would be used to pay out their freeze interest.
- Also, a discretionary family trust for their children could become the new common shareholder instead of having the children subscribe for the shares directly. That might be a better plan than

having Willy own the shares personally at this point. Down the road, the trust could distribute the shares to them equally or in some other percentage.

- There is no immediate personal tax cost to Bill and Margaret on a freeze. Tax would be paid by them only when they receive redemption proceeds on the freeze shares.

"Now, that's a plan," Bill said. "But what about my employees? I really want them to pay for the shares rather than get them for a nominal amount. How will the freeze work for them?"

"Good question, Bill."

The financial advisor explained that separate classes of new common shares could be created as part of the freeze. For instance, Class B common non-voting shares could be issued to key employees at a price which reflected market values. These shares would be separate and distinct from Class A common voting shares, reserved solely for family members. That way, only family members would own the voting shares, while key employees could hold participating non-voting growth shares.

The company could also lend employees the funds to acquire these Class B common shares and they could repay their loans over time by applying bonuses or dividends paid to them as shareholders. That way, they acquire their interest through performance which they earn or pay for over time.

"Hmmm, sounds pretty good! I think this is the way to go."

IN SUMMARY

This chapter examined issues which are common to many mature family-run companies—how to transition to the next generation.

The discussion focused on the tax and non-tax matters typical to most such companies and examined two possible solutions. The first solution involved a simple direct sale of the business, while the latter reviewed the concept of an estate freeze. Share ownership by employees was discussed briefly with a short analysis of that alternative.

THINGS YOU NEED TO KNOW

- Determine the approximate fair market value of your business. Your company is one of your most significant assets and it is important to gauge its value, relative to your overall net worth, in terms of any plan to transition to your children.

- Determine the tax consequences of selling or transitioning your shares at their current value. It is prudent to determine your potential estate tax liability on death and to plan to fund such liability (i.e. life insurance).

- Review and examine with your financial advisor the basic strategies to transition your company (sale, estate freeze).

QUESTIONS YOU NEED TO ASK

- What is my company worth today?
- Are my children interested in share ownership? Are they right for the company?
- Can I equalize my estate in other ways if I don't leave my children equal shares in the business?
- How much tax would my estate have to pay if I leave my company shares to my children?
- Are my employees interested in share ownership? Are they a necessary component for the business transition, even if my children become shareholders? Can I remunerate key employees in other ways?

THINGS YOU NEED TO DO

- Determine what your company is worth today.
- Create a plan and a timeline to facilitate transition.
- Discuss and involve key employees, your children and your financial advisors in any significant transitional plan.

DECISIONS YOU NEED TO MAKE

- Decide how you will begin the transition process. Identify the key people (employees, children) and the key strategies with the help of your financial advisors.
- Decide whether employee ownership makes sense for your company. There are pros and cons to this alternative.

MASTER YOUR INVESTMENT IN THE FAMILY BUSINESS
The Estate Freeze—When is it Time?

TIPS

- Communication with your successors, advisors and key employees is vital to the transition process. Be aware that a good plan takes time and effort to implement. Be prepared to invest considerable effort to make it happen.

- Review your will in conjunction with your business transition plan to ensure that the tax and legal implications resulting from an untimely demise dovetail with your succession plan.

- Seek competent tax and valuation advice. Implementing an estate freeze is complex.

TRAPS

- Be aware that the business succession plan may not always go as expected. The transition to children or employees can sometimes cause a financial upheaval. Be sure that your estate freeze gives you a "back door" if you need to step in and take control.

Principle Mastery: Design your business succession and estate planning strategies with enough flexibility to meet your time expectations and survive uncertain future events.

CHAPTER 9

Planning for Crisis Situations: Illness, Family Strife and Breakups

Hope for the best, but plan for the worst. (ENGLISH PROVERB)

Jason and Darren were 11 holes into their weekly golf game. Jason, aged 48, and Darren, aged 50, were both business owners and were discussing the news of the week as they negotiated through the course on a hot and sunny day.

Darren spoke of a friend whose son had taken over the family business two years ago so that his father, who was recovering from a knee operation, could be less involved in the business. The arrangement worked out well for the first six months, but when economic conditions worsened, the working capital of the business dropped dramatically and the son, who lacked the knowledge and experience to address the matter, was faced with a business that was nearly bankrupt. The father was forced to return to the business to sort out what had become a desperate situation.

"Can you imagine that?" Darren asked Jason.

Jason told Darren about his neighbours, Maria and Jack, who were going through a bitter divorce. Maria had replaced her father in managing her family's textiles business and her husband Jack had taken on the job of production manager. With the divorce proceedings in full swing, Jack was taking the position that he should be compensated for a portion of the significant growth of the business, much to the dismay of Maria's family. Jason commented that, with all of the emotional angst, concerns regarding the financial future of the business seemed too much to bear.

The two friends moved to the twelfth hole. It was mid-afternoon and the sun was very hot. Jason took off his hat, wiped his brow, and stepped up to the tee box. He suddenly felt tense and exhausted by the heat. He fell to the ground, and as he gasped for breath and looked up at the clear summer sky, he wondered, "What is happening to me?"

THE ISSUES

Luckily for Jason, he was just dehydrated. He recovered after drinking lots of fluids and resting, but what if the reason for his collapse had been more serious? Darren and Jason were right to be concerned about all of the situations they discussed. There are many crisis situations that not only pose a risk to business leaders and their families, but can put the business at risk as well. These situations can be tragic to individuals when they occur and can compound the stress and loss of the situation by impacting the family's economic well-being at a time when they are at their most vulnerable. Planning ahead for the unexpected can help.

Let's consider some of these crisis situations, in terms of how they can impact individuals, families, and the business.

- **Illness.** As family business leaders age, it is not uncommon for illnesses to arise, sometimes of a serious nature. An illness could force a family business leader out of the business for a period of time or permanently. If there is no one within the business who can competently fill this role, the business faces the risk of significant damage, or may simply grind to a halt.

- **Death.** The death of a family business leader, particularly when it is sudden or unexpected, is not only devastating to the family, it also puts the future of the business and the family's economic well-being at risk. In the absence of a clear succession plan, family members will struggle to determine the best approach to go forward, and may be forced to make important decisions at a time when they are at their weakest. Situations such as this can represent a double loss to the family: losing a beloved family member, and also losing the strength, direction, and financial performance of the business.

- **Divorce.** The end of marital and common-law relationships among family members is a painful distraction, and can represent an even greater risk to the business. In the absence of proper planning and written agreements, individuals outside of the family (such as Jack) can take the position that they are entitled to earnings or an ownership position in the business, which is a risk for the family. This can be the case not only for the family business leader, but also in the case of family members who may be less involved in the business (i.e., children, siblings, etc.). These types of situations can take a considerable amount of time and energy to sort out, particularly in the absence of documentation and agreements, and the business can be held captive by the situation.

- **Conflict.** It is not unusual for family businesses to be impacted by the ups and downs of family relationships; this is particularly true for businesses that have not evolved to the professional management approach of a Market Driven Family Business. The risk to the business in this type of situation is that the business may function poorly, due to the distraction of family conflicts and power struggles, and may create uncertainty in terms of how key roles and responsibilities will be fulfilled. It is very difficult for non-family members to deal with the uncertainty and unclear direction that may occur in these situations and many may opt to leave for a more stable environment.

- **Insufficient Succession Planning.** Some family business leaders may fail to properly plan and implement a succession plan, a mistake that may escalate soon after the succession event occurs, thereby creating a crisis situation for the business.

Do you remember the concept of "imaginary succession"? In this case, the family business leader may have done only a superficial job in terms of developing a succession plan, may have failed to consistently enforce expectations in terms of what family members have to achieve in order to take over the business, or perhaps failed to engage a qualified business advisor to ask the hard questions and keep the process on track. The result is that a "succession" transaction may occur, however, the successor does not have the skills, resources, or ability to take the business forward, which could lead to a disastrous situation. The family business leader may have to step in, try to save the business, and if the business can be salvaged, start all over again in terms of developing a proper succession plan.

- **Ineffective Family Business Leader.** In some situations, the business may grow or evolve to the point where the family business leader no longer has the ability or desire to keep up with the increasing requirements of the position. This may occur in situations where the business is operating in a technical industry, where the technology and industry requirements have increased dramatically. If the family business leader does not recognize or is not willing to recognize the gap between their skills and ability and what is required to successfully lead the organization, the market position of the business is at risk. The real damage is done when this type of situation is allowed to continue for a prolonged period of time, after which the business may not be able to recover.

When the family business leader is lost to the business, for a period of time or permanently, it can be devastating to a business, especially a Lifestyle Family Business, where there may not be adequately qualified and experienced members of the business who can take over the role of the family business leader. The risk is that the business will be significantly damaged, perhaps irreparably, in terms of both financial position and reputation. This is a key reason why migration to the professional management approach exemplified by a Market Driven Family Business is so important.

THE SOLUTIONS

There are various solutions to consider when addressing people-related crisis situations and their potential impact on the business. The objective is to plan accordingly so that the business can be safeguarded from these situations as much as possible, thereby enabling it to continue to operate without significant interruption or harm.

Let's consider some of the things that a family business leader should do in order to protect the business from these types of situations.

Operate as a Market Driven Family Business

As previously discussed, Market Driven Family Businesses have the objective of successfully competing in the marketplace and this cannot occur without a competent and well-qualified staff and management group.

This approach incorporates the concept of professional management, whether it is provided by family or non-family members. Having a professional management framework is an important requirement to successfully grow a business, as it provides the necessary depth and capacity for growth. These types of organizations are able to spread responsibilities across various individuals, which helps to mitigate the risk that arises from loss of an individual. Market Driven Family Businesses typically have the depth and skills that are required to continue to operate during crisis situations, and adopting this type of approach is important for safeguarding the business, as well as reducing the dependency of the business on the family business leader.

Document Your Company Policies and Procedures

In an era when the "street smarts" of a business can walk out the door in text messages, emails, and other virtual networking activities, it is more important than ever to document operating policies and procedures in a central location in order to formally communicate the necessary instructions to run every aspect of the business.

This is particularly important, in terms of ensuring that the core knowledge and processes for managing the business are not simply "in the head" of the family business leader, which can represent a significant risk to the business in the absence of that person. This type of formal documentation represents value to a successor or potential acquirer of the business, and also mitigates the risk of a failed succession. In short, it ensures that the core "business know-how" is preserved in the business and becomes part of it for the long term.

In addition, the use of employment agreements is an important mechanism for safeguarding policies and procedures, by way of confidentiality, adherence to policy, and code of conduct requirements. In the age of virtual information, where information and documents can be easily circulated with little thought to the consequences, this approach can help to clarify expectations and safeguard important business information.

Have a Formal Succession Plan

It is critical to have a plan that can be implemented in crisis situations, including a formal succession plan. A succession plan not only ensures that timely and appropriate steps are taken to continue the operations of the business in the absence of the family business leader, it also makes your wishes known so that family members do not have to struggle with determining the right course of action at what could be a time when they are at their most vulnerable.

In the event of illness, death, or any other situation that gives rise to the absence of the family business leader for a prolonged or permanent period of time, a succession plan will provide direction in a number of key areas, including:

- How implementation of the succession plan will occur and who is responsible for monitoring implementation
- Who will take over the family business leader's role
- How vacancies of the person(s) who took over the family business leader's role should be addressed (i.e., other employees within the business may be identified to assume these roles, etc.)
- How ownership positions should be adjusted (i.e., in the case of death or disability, the family business leader's shares may be transferred to others or a family trust, etc.)

- Shifting or re-distribution of responsibilities between various positions
- Training and professional development requirements
- Legal requirements, in terms of transfer of ownership, signing authorities, appointment and resignation of offices, etc.
- Steps to take regarding transfer or sale of the business, etc.

Depending on the situation, the succession plan may make reference to the family business leader's will. It is important to recognize that the purpose of the will is to address matters relating to the decedent's estate, and although it may be related to the succession plan, it is important for the business to "own" the succession plan so that the issues of the business are defined. The business must be treated as a distinct and separate entity, so that its operations do not get bogged down in processes that relate to the estate, to the detriment of the business.

Although the "spirit" of the business may be an extension of the family business leader, the business is a separate entity from a legal and tax perspective. The business could have other shareholders and partners who have legal rights under a shareholders' or partnership agreement, and as a result, the business must be sufficiently structured to stand on its own, in terms of matters of management, decision making, and succession, to name a few.

Have Proper Legal Documentation and Agreements

It is not uncommon for business owners to take the position that, generally speaking, they do not need legal advice. Complaints that legal matters are complicated, costly, and of little value are typical. However, such an attitude fails to consider that, in the absence of competent legal advice and documentation, the business and ultimately the family's financial future are facing significant risk.

Areas such as shareholders' agreements, proper share documentation, employment agreements, and articles and bylaws are just some examples of areas where businesses should get qualified legal advice. Financings and business transactions, such as mergers, acquisitions, and sale of business are specialized areas where businesses should not try to "save money" by going it alone. The result of poor or no advice can be far more costly than the price of getting good advice.

Family business leaders should speak with their legal advisor to understand the implications and risks that may arise from the breakdown of marital or common-law relationships, in the case of themselves and other family members that are shareholders in the business. If proper steps are not taken, the business may be exposed to unnecessary risk, in terms of non-family members having reasonable claims against the business, which could lead to additional costs and strife within the business and the family. Use of pre-marital agreements, for example, provides the opportunity to safeguard the business from this type of situation, and the best time to negotiate is when people "like each other".

Another area to address is key person insurance. The business may obtain life, disability, or other forms of insurance for the family business leader or other key positions in the business. In this type of situation, the business is named as the beneficiary of the policy and, in the event of death or disability, the policy would make a payment to the business. This type of coverage can provide resources for implementing the succession process, bringing in interim professional management, or settling the family business leader's ownership position with the estate, depending on the specific structural arrangement. A qualified insurance professional can provide possible structures and coverage arrangements for consideration by the family business leader.

Recognize that the Best Interest of the Business Must Prevail

Most people can probably think of family businesses that they are familiar with or have heard about where conflict amongst family members is a typical occurrence. Whether it is a case of squabbling siblings, children who do not agree with how a parent manages the business, or spouses or common law partners who do not see eye-to-eye, the business typically suffers from the slings and arrows of these situations.

The bottom line is that the best interest of the business must prevail; otherwise, the family is putting their own financial future at risk, as well as that of other family members. Family businesses can be a double-edged sword: they benefit from the camaraderie and teamwork of family, but they are also vulnerable to the impact of close, personal relationships, which can be characterized by a gamut of emotions and personal history.

The solutions to successfully managing through these types of situations can vary, but the following key points can help guide family business leaders in times of conflict between family members in the business:

- **Re-enforce the Market Driven Family Business approach.** This will focus the business and family members *outward*, on doing what is necessary to successfully compete in the marketplace, instead of *inward*, where there is an overemphasis on the internal issues of the business, including the basis of family conflict, which may or may not be relevant to the marketplace. Qualified non-family members, especially those at a senior level, can provide a much-needed "reality check" to situations where family members are not focusing on what is important in terms of running the business. Professional management can provide the safety net when family dynamics spiral out of control.

  However, this will only work well if the owner takes the time to select, instruct, and guide the transition team. Many owners know how to make "widgets" well, but they don't know how to teach people what they know. This requires a special kind of mentorship and guidance from the family business leader.

- **Fix bad situations.** This may sound obvious, but it is not uncommon for conflicts and poor performance to continue within a family business for a prolonged period of time, with family business leader simply "looking the other way", avoiding the problem, or hoping that the situation will change. This is not likely; in fact, the opposite is true in most cases.

  As previously mentioned, members of the business, especially non-family members, are looking to the family business leader to resolve problems. Situations of conflict and poor performance not only damage the ability of the business to operate well, they also reduce the motivation of those in the business who are performing well, leading to a bad environment and departing staff members.

Resolving a bad situation with a family member can include termination of employment and share buyout or other approaches. Some situations can be resolved by the parties agreeing to divide the business into separate entities, or providing the opportunity for a family member to pursue business in a separate division or related company. This approach may provide enough separation for the parties to eliminate the day-to-day conflict, without sacrificing the business and its position in the marketplace in the process.

Recognizing that there are approaches to address family conflict is important, as if this does not occur, the business, and ultimately the family, will suffer. Going forward in another manner is not necessarily a bad thing; it may simply be what is necessary to allow the business to continue to be successful in changing times.

Separate the Life Cycle of the Business From the Life Cycle of the Family Business Leader

In a lot of ways, this is what professional management and succession planning seek to do—reduce the dependence on the family business leader and create some depth within the organization to both protect and move the business forward.

Some businesses really are the family business leader. Think of many Lifestyle Family Businesses, or the example of Mary Ann in Chapter 3. The problem with this approach is that growth is constrained to what the family business leader alone can do, skills are limited, and the business is at risk should the family business leader not be able to be active in the business. This situation is a risk to the family's financial future, and puts a limit on what can be achieved from all of the time and effort that the family business leader has invested in building the business.

Thinking of the family business leader as an integral part of the business, but also taking the steps to provide the business with its own life cycle for operations and growth, allows the family business leader to recognize what the business needs to become and stay successful. This includes professional management, incorporating skills and experience that the family business leader does not possess, and other critical components that are required for the business to successfully compete in the market-place. A qualified business advisor can be helpful in building the necessary framework to separate the life cycle of the family business leader from the life cycle of the business, and can be a good resource in terms of keeping the process on track.

In the Case of Disaster, Get Help

If a family business is operating as a Market Driven Family Business or has a sound succession plan, it is in a far better position to face crisis situations. However, it will still be challenged in times of crisis. Crisis situations are never easy, and in the case of a family business that is less or poorly prepared, or has undergone an unsuccessful leadership transition, the business may have deteriorated to a point where it may not be able to be salvaged.

A qualified business advisor can objectively help to get the business back on track, bringing experience and perspective to wade through the emotional aspects of the situation. Since they are not a family member, they are well equipped to look at the situation for what it is, as opposed to dwelling on family member personal situations. They may not be able to fix every problem, or salvage every situation, but are likely the best resource to try.

Corrective action may include steps such as terminating members of the business who are not fulfilling their role, bringing in interim professional management to hold key positions, revising a failed succession plan, or even selling part or all of the business. These solutions may not be ideal, but they should, at a minimum, salvage at least some of the wealth of the business for the family's sake.

If this sounds depressing, that may be because you have recognized that there are many things that a family business leader could have done in order to avoid ending up in this type of situation. Reflecting on the areas that have been discussed thus far in this book is certainly worthwhile!

IN SUMMARY

Several people-related crises may plague the business during its life cycle, with family conflict, divorce, illness, and premature death all representing potential threats. Family businesses may outgrow the management skills of their owner or the actively participating family members, or may experience a failed succession attempt. Many of these situations can be managed to a successful result by way of proactive discussion and decision making that preserves not only relationships, but the investment in the family business as well.

Solutions to mitigate the impact of crisis situations include operating as a Market Driven Family Business and having a formal succession plan and proper documentation and agreements. Separating the life cycle of the family business leader from the life cycle of the business can be achieved by way of professional management and a sound succession plan, and is a key component in recognizing the business as a distinct entity that is not solely reliant on the family business leader. This approach provides the basis for stability of operations and longevity, in times of crisis or otherwise.

A qualified business advisor can be a useful resource for defining the components of the business life cycle, keeping it on track, and salvaging disaster situations. Even more important, there are many things that the family business leader can do proactively to avoid catastrophic situations.

THINGS YOU NEED TO KNOW

- People-related crisis situations have the potential to derail a family business and can represent a significant threat.

- Operating as a Market Driven Family Business and having a sound succession plan can greatly mitigate the impact of crisis situations on a family business.

- A good succession plan not only helps the business to continue to operate and move forward in a timely manner, it also communicates the wishes of the family business leader, eliminating the need for family members to struggle to determine what may be the best course of action at a time when they are experiencing heightened emotions or loss.

- Separating the life cycle of the family business leader from the life cycle of the business can bring focus to what the business needs to do to achieve stability and longevity, creating the opportunity to build wealth over a longer period of time. The two life cycles need not be the same.

- Proper documentation, including policies and procedures, as well as legal agreements, are required to protect the business from crisis situations, particularly in the instance of the breakdown of marital or common-law relationships.

- In the case of disaster, get help. A qualified professional advisor can objectively help to get the business back on track.

QUESTIONS YOU NEED TO ASK

- Does the business have a sound succession plan that can be implemented in times of crisis?

- Does the business have appropriate documentation and agreements that protect it from crisis situations, such as the breakdown of marital and common-law relationships?

- Does the business have adequate key person insurance coverage that could provide proceeds to cover the costs of succession or interim management in a crisis situation?

- Are there family members within the business who are no longer qualified to perform their role, due to technical advancements or lack of interest?

- Are there conflicts among family members within the business that need to be resolved?

- Does the business have its own life cycle, or is it dependent upon the family business leader?

THINGS YOU NEED TO DO

- Review the key agreements of your business and determine if enhancements or updates are required.

- Meet with your legal advisor to discuss update of agreements or additional risk areas to be addressed.

- Review your succession plan to ensure that it addresses all areas that would require attention in a crisis situation.

- Meet with a qualified insurance professional to determine if key person insurance should be incorporated into your business and review the options for doing so.

- Address any existing family conflicts in the business and explore options for resolution, including termination, splitting of the business, or agreement to permanently resolve the matter.

- If your business is currently in a crisis situation and not managing well, get professional help from a qualified business advisor.

DECISIONS YOU NEED TO MAKE

- If you do not have a sound succession plan, you must develop one, including deciding how the business will move forward in your absence. This includes identifying your successor(s) or indicating if the business is to be transferred or sold upon your departure.

- In the event of an existing family conflict, the best interest of the business must prevail, which includes resolving the matter. As the family business leader, you must determine the best course of action.

MASTER YOUR INVESTMENT IN THE FAMILY BUSINESS

Planning for Crisis Situations: Illness, Family Strife and Breakups

TIPS

- Documenting your wishes for the business in your absence, by way of a sound succession plan or other documentation, makes your wishes clear and takes a considerable burden off family members.

- The best sign of a family business leader's success is when a team has been built that can competently take the business forward, in times of planned succession or crisis. A needy business represents weakness and missed potential.

- The professional management approach of a Market Driven Family Business can provide the safety net when family dynamics spiral out of control.

TRAPS

- Some family business leaders may have a need for the business to be dependent on them. This is not in the best interest of the business, and speaks more about the personal needs of the family business leader than the needs of the business.

- Regarding legal advice as an unnecessary cost of little value is a naïve approach. Sound legal advice, in terms of proper agreements, documentation, and advice to guide decision making can save a business from the financial ruin that can ensue in the absence of such advice.

Principle Mastery: When you view the business as a separate entity, rather than an extension of yourself, the opportunity exists for the business to move forward in a manner that is in its own best interest, and to the ultimate benefit of the family.

CHAPTER 10

Planning for the Founder's Tax Efficient Retreat

Never spend your money before you have it. THOMAS JEFFERSON

George and his wife Lynn have owned their trucking company for over thirty years. George first started out doing long hauls for one of the big national trucking companies. He met Lynn at one of his favorite truck stops and the rest was history! They have a couple of kids (now married) who are both university educated. The kids don't know anything about the trucking industry and never did get involved in the family business.

George and Lynn both know that when the time comes to give up the business they will probably have to sell to one of their big competitors. While it sticks in his craw to do this, George does want to maximize the after-tax wealth he built up in the business over the last 30 years. George and Lynn also want to maintain the lifestyle that the family business afforded them.

While they aren't selling today, George knows that the transition of his business to another owner is probably just a few years away. His company owns a warehouse and distribution building, some trucks and equipment, and holds the trucking rights to some key routes in western Canada.

George has always prudently used good professional advice over the years and he decided to give his financial advisor a call to talk things over.

THE ISSUES

George's financial advisor, Ed Sloan, identified three main issues to help George and Lynn think about their future, and that of the business:

- How to prepare the business for sale
- The difference between a sale of assets and a sale of shares
- How to plan for income continuance after the sale of the business

Preparing the Business for Sale

George and Lynn's business was always profitable. However, for tax planning purposes, George had paid out bonuses to himself and Lynn over the years. This reduced the corporate profit for tax purposes. A prospective buyer who looked at the financial statements might not readily understand that the profits were actually higher than shown. Also, George and Lynn liked to travel and they were able to combine business with their personal life. A number of convention and trade show expenses reduced the company profits in the financial statements.

Ed suggested George and Lynn contact their accountant to prepare a report normalizing the corporate profits over the last four or five years, with a view to placing an Estimate of Value on the overall company. After all, in getting ready for a sale, it is critically important that the owner know the level of profits the company can generate, and what the company is worth.

Sale of Assets Versus Sale of Shares

Next, Ed asked George whether he had thought much about how the sale would be structured.

"No, I haven't," replied George. "Isn't it as simple as the buyer writing us a cheque?"

"Well, that's true," his financial advisor chuckled. "However, what you should know is that there's a very different tax treatment if the company sells its assets (such as the building, trucks, trucking rights, etc.) versus you and Lynn selling the shares of the company."

He explained that a sale of shares of their company would result in a taxable capital gain to them personally.

"However, you and Lynn will each be eligible to claim the $750,000 Lifetime Capital Gains Exemption on the sale of your shares. If, on the other hand, the company sells assets, there will be tax payable within the company, and also a second level of tax when you distribute the sale proceeds by way of dividend."

Ed also warned the couple to be careful about signing a "non-compete" agreement.

"There can be adverse tax consequences arising from its tax treatment."

"Shoot! That's not good," bellowed George. "Isn't there a way to fix that?"

"Well, that leads us to the third issue," Ed responded.

Planning for income continuance after the sale. Part of getting ready for a sale requires the setting up of "pots" or "pools" of cash from which the business owners can draw when they retire.

"That way," Ed winked, "you and Lynn can continue to enjoy your golden years as you 'truck on down the highway!'"

"I'm listening," George grinned.

"First, you and Lynn have been working for the company for over 30 years. There are a couple of ways that you can stash some cash in a plan and have the company take a deduction now or when the contribution is made. I'll explain those later," Ed added.

"Second, you might want to consider holding on to that building you have. It's a great location and real estate is a solid investment. We should look at ways in which you can sell the business and still hold on to the real estate."

"Lastly, we'll want to explore the ways you can continue your health care and employee benefits plan. You and Lynn both like to travel a lot and I don't think that will change after you sell the business."

"Okay," George said, "let's hear what you've got!" Lynn smiled in agreement.

THE SOLUTIONS

The financial advisor began to outline a few solutions for George and Lynn, but cautioned that the best approach is a team approach—one that included the couple's accountant and lawyer.

"To master your investment in the family business, now is the time to work with your tax accountant and lawyer, whose role is to provide you with the great advice you need to help you properly position the company for a sale down the road."

Specifically, Ed outlined the following issues, which should be considered when planning for the founder's tax efficient retreat:

- Preparing the Business for Sale
- Sale of Shares vs. Sale of Assets
- Planning for Retirement Income
    - Registered Retirement Savings Plan (RRSP)
    - Individual pension plan
    - Retirement Compensation Arrangements (RCAs)
    - Generating tax efficient investment income
    - Using retiring allowances
    - Health care and employee benefits plans
    - Pension income splitting

Preparing the Business for Sale

It is important for the founder to position the investment in the family business to maximize the after-tax proceeds of a sale. The $750,000 Lifetime Capital Gains Deduction enables a shareholder to realize that amount of capital gains, without paying tax, providing that the shares qualify at the time of the sale or disposition. In order to qualify, the shares must meet certain tests at the date of sale, as well as for the immediately preceding 24 months.

"Your tax accountant is the best person to fully explain the rules in this area," explained their financial advisor.

"Also, the use of the $750,000 Lifetime Capital Gains Deduction can be multiplied by involving other family members as shareholders of the company, either directly or indirectly through a trust. Your two children, though not actively involved in the trucking company, could be introduced as shareholders," Ed suggested. "By doing so, you will be able to expand the use of the $750,000 Lifetime Capital Gains Deduction, and thereby multiply your tax savings on a future sale of the company."

"Taking the steps to do so," he explained, "requires careful planning and possible restructuring well in advance of a contemplated sale. In particular, a business owner must be careful to obtain and implement proper valuations when introducing new family members as shareholders. Otherwise, CRA can invoke serious taxes and penalties for failing to implement these ownership changes properly."

It became clear to the couple that an astute tax accountant and lawyer should be engaged to properly plan, structure and implement an estate freeze, and to introduce new family members as shareholders in the family business. Fortunately, Lynn and George had worked with their trusted advisory team (including their lawyer and accountant) for many years on such matters. They made a mental note to re-visit these issues and to ask a few pertinent questions about their family share structure. That Capital Gains Deduction was certainly too good to pass by, and clearly their ticket to a future of fun and travel!

Sale of Shares vs. Sale of Assets

In most cases, the founder and the family shareholders would prefer to sell the shares of the company, as opposed to having the company sell its operating assets and business goodwill.

"That's because of the tax-free treatment on the first $750,000 of capital gains, right?" asked Lynn.

"Exactly," replied their financial advisor. "The $750,000 Lifetime Capital Gains Deduction applies to individual taxpayers, and not in respect of assets sold within a corporation. However, sometimes a prospective purchaser is not willing to acquire the shares of the company and will only agree to purchase the operating assets and goodwill. This can be for a number of reasons, including concerns about assuming the prior liabilities of the target company, inheriting its existing employees, and acquiring assets with a potential deferred tax liability."

"What do you mean about that last point?" queried George.

"Well," Ed continued, "when a purchaser acquires the shares of an existing company, the cost of the assets owned within the corporation are not 'stepped-up' for tax purposes, even though the price agreed upon for the shares may reflect the underlying fair market value of such assets. Consequently, if the new owner subsequently sells those assets, the company he just acquired would be facing a tax bill on any capital gains or recaptured capital cost allowance realized on the sale.

"That might be the situation in your case, George," he added. "The warehouse and distribution building you own within the company have been almost fully depreciated for tax purposes, and those assets would generate a significant tax bill if sold. They probably would present a problem to a prospective purchaser if you wanted to sell the shares of the company.

"On the other hand, a sale of assets can potentially result in 'double tax' when you flow the money out to you personally."

"Why is that?" asked Lynn.

"Well, that's because the assets sold by your company will be subject to tax first when sold, and then a second level of tax will apply when funds are distributed by the corporation to you personally. Not only that, the corporate tax which applies on a sale of assets can differ, depending on the type of asset sold.

"Depreciable capital assets, such as your trucks, buildings and office equipment will generally create recaptured capital cost allowance— income which is fully subject to tax. Sale proceeds in excess of the cost of capital property will result in the corporation being subject to capital gains taxes. In this case, only half of the gain is subject to tax, while the other half is treated as a special surplus item and added to the corporation's capital dividend account—CDA".

Lynn and George looked blankly at each other at this point.

"The CDA of a company can be distributed as a special tax-free dividend," Ed explained before going on. "Finally, a sale of goodwill or some other intangible is treated as a disposition of eligible capital property—ECP— with the result that half of such ECP is subject to tax as ordinary business income of the corporation. The other half effectively increases the corporation's CDA account.

"Good planning can help to minimize the impact of these two levels of taxes. Once again, you should consult your tax accountant on the matter, or we can set up a meeting to chat about this together. Ideally, separate calculations should be performed to determine how much would be realized on an after-tax basis for a sale of shares versus a sale of assets. Such calculations will give you the necessary information to evaluate a potential offer from a buyer."

This plan seemed to sit well with Lynn and George.

"Also, a sale of assets has tax compliance consequences—you will continue to have ongoing filing requirements for the company. Just because the assets are sold doesn't mean that you can wash your hands of the CRA. Corporate taxes, GST and financial statement preparation will still be an ongoing requirement.

"The other issue to be aware of," the financial advisor cautioned, "is liability on employee termination. If a prospective buyer acquires the assets of your business and not the shares, your company may still have an ongoing liability with respect to any claims arising on employee dismissal or termination, which is quite likely if the buyer does not continue that employment relationship. You will be responsible for paying severance and vacation pay in that instance.

"In a nutshell, while a sale of assets is a lot cleaner for the buyer, it can leave you with a lot of issues to deal with," Ed concluded. "It's best to try to sell the shares instead, if these issues are important. Otherwise, they must be taken into account in a higher selling price."

"That's a lot of information to process," said George. "Can you boil that down to the pros and cons of each situation?"

"Sure. Here goes," responded Ed, as he outlined the following summary of pros and cons on his whiteboard.

Sale of Shares

	Pros	Cons
Share Purchase Agreement	• Preferred by vendor	• Complicated
Use of $750,000 Lifetime Capital Gains Deduction ("LCGD")	• Tax free proceeds	• Tax complications • Corporation must qualify • Redundant assets to remove
Ability to multiply use of $750,000 LCGD	• Additional tax free proceeds to family	• Risks associated with other family members as shareholders • Improper valuation on estate freeze
Ongoing Compliance	• Reporting in year of sale; otherwise terminates	• N/A

Sale of Assets

	Pros	Cons
Asset Purchase Agreement	• Straight forward; easy to structure • Preferred by purchaser (step up in ACB of assets)	• Potential ongoing liabilities to vendor • Exposure to creditors, employee termination issues
Taxation	• Ability to access tax-free CDA if sale properly structured	• Potential for double taxation
Ongoing Compliance	• N/A	• Reporting continues until company dissolved

"Can you tell us about non-compete clauses and management agreements," George asked. "How do these items factor into a sale?"

"Generally, the buyer will require the principal shareholders—George, that would be you and Lynn—to sign an agreement not to compete with the purchaser in the same or similar business within a prescribed geographical region in which the business operated for a specified number of years. Very often, part of the consideration for the agreed price is earmarked or allocated to the non-compete.

"But be careful," warned Ed. "Proceeds allocated to a non-compete will be treated as ordinary income and subject to tax on the full amount, unless a joint election is filed by both the purchaser and vendor to treat the amount as part of the sale proceeds of the business. The latter is preferential, as capital gains treatment is afforded on the joint election.

"Also, George, the purchaser may want to retain your services during a transitional period and suggest that management fees could be paid to you and Lynn," he added. "Where this is the case, be careful to ensure that a bona fide management contract is in place, and that it is clear that the services provided are that of an independent contractor, and not one which could be construed as a contract of employment services. If the agreement creates an employee-employer relationship there will be less favourable tax treatment afforded to the deductions which you can claim against that income.

"Finally, be aware that the purchaser may wish to re-characterize part of the sales price into tax-deductible management fees. This is clearly not to the benefit of the vendor as it results in such management fee income becoming fully taxable to the recipient, as opposed to receiving proceeds on the sale of the company, subject to capital gains treatment."

Planning for Retirement Income

Getting the business ready for sale also includes setting up one or more savings plans designed specifically to accumulate your wealth and build capital for retirement.

Lynn and George were particularly interested in this subject area, as they had many plans for enjoying their much-deserved time off.

"There are a number of different ways to do so and various tax-deferred plans that can be utilized, in order to maximize your retirement wealth," the advisor stated, before launching into a summary of the key planning strategies.

Registered Retirement Savings Plan (RRSP)

The couple's financial advisor pointed out the benefits of utilizing RRSPs.

"You should continue to make contributions to your RRSPs, based on your earned income—that is, the salaries paid to you from the trucking company. These contributions are tax-deductible to you and grow tax-deferred within the RRSP. In taxation years where you enjoy a significant profit in your company, you will continue paying a bonus to reduce corporate profits and then use that bonus to fund or top up your RRSPs to the extent of your RRSP deduction room.

"The net effect of this strategy is that the company gets a tax deduction for the bonus, and the funds end up in your RRSP," Ed explained. "There is no immediate net tax cost to you! Later when you reach the age of 65 there are some interesting income splitting opportunities that will save you even more taxes. But we will get to that later."

Individual Pension Plan

An individual pension plan (IPP) is effectively a defined benefit pension plan (similar to a Registered Pension Plan or RPP.) Owners of a family-run company can set one up, much in the same manner as a big corporation. The IPP is the way in which private family run companies can access pension benefits in a fashion similar to that of an RPP.

"The IPP will pay a pension to you based on a percentage of what you've been earning over the last 30 years and it can also be inflation-indexed. The maximum pension is calculated as followed:

- 2 percent of your earnings per annum
- times the number of years worked,
- to a maximum of 2 times CPP pensionable earnings.

"Since you have not contributed to such a plan at all," said their financial advisor, "your company can make a past-service contribution to fund up the necessary capital in order to sustain a pension to you on retirement.

A similar IPP can be set up for Lynn, or alternatively, the company can set up a joint IPP for you both."

"Here are the advantages in doing so," he explained, as he continued his overview on the white board in the boardroom:

- You remove excess cash from the trucking company and create a tax-deferred pool of money you can draw upon when you retire;
- The company is entitled to a tax deduction for the past-service contribution, plus all on-going current contributions; and
- The value of the IPP and the pension benefits you can build will generally exceed the pension benefits you can obtain from a money-purchase RRSP plan.

"However," Ed pointed out, "an IPP contribution can be made in the year of sale, particularly if the company is selling assets and triggering a significant tax-event. That way, you can lower the taxable income of the company resulting from a gain in the year of sale, and stash some cash in an IPP for your golden years!"

"That sounds perfect," said George and Lynn, almost in unison. "What else do we need to know?"

Retirement Compensation Arrangements (RCAs)

"Another avenue is to set up an RCA—a Retirement Compensation Arrangement. It enables a company to make a tax-deductible contribution to your retirement plan, provided that 50% of the contribution goes to CRA as a refundable tax credit."

"Whoa!" said George. "Why would I pay a 50% tax to the CRA?" Lynn thought that was a pretty good question, too.

"Well, a number of reasons, George," replied Ed.

"First, the full contribution to the RCA is deductible to the payor company. That deduction can be particularly useful in a taxation year when assets are sold within the company, and there would otherwise be a substantial amount of corporate tax to pay," he explained.

"Second, the 50% tax is refundable when the RCA makes a distribution to the annuitant. So the contribution bears a 50% prepayment of tax, which is refunded to the RCA so that a full distribution can later be made.

"In effect, the RCA is made whole again, and the entire amount contributed to the plan by the company can now be paid out to the annuitant as pension income at a later date. Then, you pay tax on the distribution only at the marginal rate you are in when you receive the income. It's a way to build up a pot of cash—particularly on a sale of your business—and perhaps do a bit better on the overall tax cost when you draw on the funds.

"But, it gets better if you decide to retire and live outside of Canada. For instance, if you take up residence in the U.S., you could receive an annuity from the RCA and be subject only to a 15% withholding tax under the Canada-US Tax Treaty. So the deferral really pays over time."

Generating Tax Efficient Investment Income

"Remember I mentioned hanging on to that building, Lynn and George?" the financial advisor reminded the couple. "Well, it can serve to generate some investment income for you and Lynn while you're away in warmer climes!"

"That sounds great," George replied. "How does that work?"

"Well, you're probably going to sell to a big national trucking company and they will be interested in your trucking routes, the business goodwill, and probably your operating assets. Buildings don't make them money, so they may be just as happy to rent the warehouse and distribution building from you. However, we should position your holdings so that the building is separate and apart from the operations in your company. Chances are, when a buyer looks at your business, they may be willing to buy the shares, but not if the building is also in the company. Removing the building just before a sale of shares can be problematic."

"Why?" asked Lynn.

"Removing the building at the time of the sale could trigger unexpected taxes, yet it may not be possible to remove the building on a tax-deferred basis immediately before a sale. If your intention is to separate the business from the real estate, you should do so well in advance of any contemplated sale. Your tax accountant will be knowledgeable about certain 'surplus-stripping' rules, and you should address this matter as part of the plan of getting your business ready for a sale.

"Also," continued Ed, "if you do it now, years before a sale, you position the operating company nicely for a potential sale of shares that are eligible for the capital gains deduction, and you can retain the building in a separate company to earn rental income. When you sell, the company that holds the building can lease out the real estate to the new buyer and continue to earn a rental income stream to supplement your retirement and lifestyle cash requirements."

"Wow!" exclaimed George. "It's sort of like a chess game. You certainly have to be thinking six moves ahead!"

"Exactly," Ed acknowledged with a smile. "There's more to think about, too. Have you considered having the company pay each of you a retiring allowance when you retire?"

Again, blank looks crossed between the couple. They were certainly interested in learning even more. Who would have thought tax planning for the business was this relevant to George and Lynn's retirement dreams?

Using Retiring Allowances
Explaining the benefits of receiving a retiring allowance also made sense to George and Lynn.

"Since both you and Lynn have worked for the trucking company for over 30 years, upon your retirement the company can make a tax-deferred transfer of a lump sum retiring allowance into your Registered Retirement Savings Plan (RRSP) and take a deduction from corporate profits, in respect of the amount contributed," counselled the advisor. "The maximum transfer is $2,000 of your retiring allowance for each year of employment before 1996, plus an additional $1,500 for each year before 1989, unless the company contributed to a Registered Pension Plan (RPP) or Deferred Profit Sharing Plan (DPSP) and the contributions vested at the time the retiring allowance was paid.

"Since your company never did set up a registered pension plan for you or Lynn, you should be able to make a substantial contribution into your RRSPs in the year of sale. If the company sells assets, this would be a great way to reduce the overall corporate tax bite. Also, these tax-deductible lump sum contributions are in addition to your normal RRSP contribution limits."

Once again, Lynn and George were fascinated, as Ed continued to outline tax efficient ways for them to benefit from their lifetime of hard work in the family business.

Health Care and Employee Benefits Plan

"I know you don't have a group plan at work right now, George," his financial advisor said.

"Yes, that's right. There are just Lynn and me, my secretary, and a book-keeper who work full-time—four of us in all. My drivers are self-employed and they take care of themselves," explained George.

"Well, you should consider implementing a plan for youself and Lynn and your two full-time employees. You can benefit by having the premiums corporately-funded and by providing for a plan to cover health, long-term disability, dental, prescription drugs, and life insurance. That would come in handy during your retirement years," added Ed.

"Plus, it would be better to fund these costs through your company. Alternatively, we could look at a 'cost-plus' plan which could provide much the same benefits as well."

"How does that work?" asked Lynn.

"Well, a cost-plus plan is an arrangement with one of the insurance companies. Your company sets up a 'private health services plan' (PHSP) that enables its employees to claim back certain qualifying medical or health costs, including dental, prescription drugs, and so on. The PHSP trustee approves the amount and submits the expense to the insurer, who then processes the claim and refunds the money to the employee."

"The insurance company then invoices the PHSP for the amount reim-bursed, plus an administration fee (usually 10%). The entire premium (cost plus admin fee) is deductible to the company. We should look into this option for you," added his financial advisor. "There are certain restrictions pertaining to the PHSP, but I think we can structure a plan for you that works."

"Moreover, when you sell the business, you will want to retain the PHSP. If we set up a separate company to hold the real estate, placing the PHSP in that company will make overall long-term sense. That way you can continue to enjoy benefits under the PHSP and continue to draw a salary or dividend from the holding company for the real estate, while retired."

This made complete sense to Lynn and George. They had been worried about their ongoing health care coverage and now could cross that concern off their list.

Pension Income Splitting

"Finally," Ed smiled, "you should ensure that you take advantage of pension income splitting elections whenever possible. Recent amendments to our Canadian federal tax legislation permit married and common-law spouses to make a joint election to 'split' certain types of qualifying pension income."

Back to the white board, the advisor outlined the qualifying pension income sources:

- RRSP or RRIF annuities, if you are age 65 or older; and
- RPP annuity income including the taxable part of life annuity payments from a superannuation or pension fund plan

Ed explained that there is no special notification required to the plan trustee. The election is made annually on each of Lynn and George's personal income tax returns, and the amount split can be changed each year, provided that no more than 50 percent of pension income is split or shifted from the pensioner spouse to the pensionee spouse.

"Also, you can elect to split your Canada Pension Plan (CPP) income in a similar fashion. You can transfer 50 percent of the benefits of one spouse or common-law partner to the other, providing that both spouses are over age 60. Doing so may result in an overall tax saving. However, the process is different. Rather than electing the split on your tax return, you must apply to the government for an assignment of benefits."

"Whew!" George whistled. "You've given us a lot to think about. I agree we should also speak to our accountant and lawyer about all of this right away. Can you help us co-ordinate a meeting and perhaps come along to make sure we get all of these terms and opportunities straight with the others?"

The advisor, of course, was honoured to do so.

IN SUMMARY

This chapter focused on planning for the founder's tax efficient retreat from operating a successful family business to navigating towards a successful sale and retirement. It examined the issues typical to many family-owned businesses and set out a number of potential solutions to address the ongoing cash flow and lifestyle requirements, as well as dealing with the matters of the sale itself on a tax-efficient basis.

Clearly, the tax issues relating to a sale of a business (assets or shares) are complex and require expert legal, accounting and tax advice. Sufficient planning may be required to re-structure corporate holdings, and to make sure that the "pots" of money required in retirement and for transition to heirs are in the right place and well protected from unnecessary taxation.

There are a variety of tax planning opportunities that exist to defer or minimize tax on a sale of the business. Usually, these initiatives go hand in hand with a strategy to provide an ongoing future source of income to the retiring founder. Hence, these initiatives need to be examined well in advance of any contemplated sale.

THINGS YOU NEED TO KNOW

- You may be entitled to the $750,000 Lifetime Capital Gains Exemption if you sell the shares of your company.
- A sale of assets versus a sale of shares creates very different tax results and very different after-tax personal cash flows.
- There are many ways to defer tax on the sale of your business, including the use of RRSPs, IPPs, RCAs, and retiring allowances.
- A corporate structure plays an integral role in the sale or retreat from your business. Ensure that you receive expert advice on your tax alternatives and leave sufficient time to re-structure, if necessary, prior to engaging a sale.

QUESTIONS YOU NEED TO ASK

- What is my company worth?
- Do my shares qualify for the $750,000 Lifetime Capital Gain Exemption?
- What is my after-tax value on a sale of shares versus a sale of assets?
- How can I defer tax on a sale of my company?
- How do I continue to augment my cash flow requirements when I sell and retire from the business?

THINGS YOU NEED TO DO

- Get a professional valuation of what your company is worth.
- Review corporate structure with your advisor and assess the changes (if any) required to plan for a sale.
- Assess advantages in setting up deferred pension and retirement plans such as an RRSP, IPP or RCA.

DECISIONS YOU NEED TO MAKE

- Decide whether you should restructure your corporate holdings to facilitate a tax-efficient sale in the future.
- Consider setting up an RRSP, IPP or an RCA, so that your company can funnel funds into the plan.
- Re-examine your health care plans as you get older, to ensure that you have adequate coverage when you retire or retreat from the business.

MASTER YOUR INVESTMENT IN THE FAMILY BUSINESS
Planning for the Founder's Tax Efficient Retreat

TIPS

- Define the issues pertaining to your company and business and develop an exit plan with your advisors.
- Act sooner rather than later. When an offer is placed on the table, it may be too late to re-structure or plan for a tax-efficient retreat.
- Seek expert tax advice. These matters are complex.

TRAPS

- Be aware of the tax provisions relating to payments made in respect of a "non-compete" clause. If a joint election is not filed, the payments would be classified as straight income to the vendor.
- Tax may be payable on recaptured capital cost allowance and capital gains within the corporation on a sale of assets. Make sure that you receive sufficient proceeds in the year of sale to cover these taxes, if the agreement calls for a "vendor take back" note. Otherwise cash flow will be negatively affected.

Principle Mastery: Planning for your retreat requires time and a plan, which affords you the flexibility to deal with the uncertain future. Start early and put the building blocks in place to ensure that your lifestyle and cash flow continue after your retreat from the business.

CHAPTER 11

When the Business
Leaves the Family

To everything there is a season. ECCLESIASTES 3:1-8

Paul, age 53, owns a frozen food distribution and warehousing company that he started 30 years ago. The company first began supplying a few local grocers and now has grown to the point where it delivers product to a large network of grocery stores citywide and across the province. Over the years, Paul has built the company into a solid frozen food distribution business, providing services to a large number of small and medium sized customers in the food industry.

Paul decided that he would like to spend another four to five years running the business and then retire. During that timeframe, he would like to see continued growth in the company, but is not thrilled with the prospect of attempting to achieve growth by building the customer base through the normal course of business. Paul does not have a clear succession plan, and although his son Shawn, aged 27, has shown a wavering interest in taking over the business, there is currently no one in the company that could succeed Paul. Despite Paul's consistent approach in terms of setting appropriate expectations for the requirements for his son to enter and eventually run the business, Shawn's commitment to fulfill the requirements has been inconsistent over the years.

Paul is considering the option of merging with another company of similar size in the frozen food distribution business, or, failing that alternative, selling to a large national distributor. He is also aware of a couple of large companies that might have an interest in acquiring his business at some point, but is not sure how to go about investigating this type of transaction. Paul is wondering if there are other options to grow his business, and would like to develop a plan over the next six months that would address his growth and succession objectives.

THE ISSUES

Paul is facing some fairly significant issues, perhaps the most challenging situation his business has ever faced, with the possible exception of the initial start-up of the business. Achieving growth in a business is never easy, but business transactions, such as mergers and acquisitions or taking on a partner with a "book of business" or established customer base, can represent both opportunities and complications.

There are two main areas of consideration in respect of such business transactions, both of which have implications for the family business leader, the family unit, and the business:

Technical Aspects of the Transaction

Since transactions like mergers, acquisitions, and the sale of a business are specialized and highly technical, most family business leaders require specialized expertise to successfully undertake a transaction of this nature. Necessary expertise may include business valuation, tax, due diligence, financing, and corporate/securities law. A qualified advisor can typically address more than one of these areas—for example, a lawyer handling the corporate/securities law requirements and some of the due diligence work. Valuation and tax advice can be obtained through accountants with specialized expertise, often by way of a firm that offers a range of professional services.

Depending on the geographic location, specialized financing advisors can be more difficult to find, particularly those whose background is in the area of venture capital or private equity investing. Advisors with experience in the banking industry are usually more readily available, but may view the opportunity differently, as their financial role is typically different than that of a venture capital/private equity investor.

Although there can be exceptions, banks tend to fill the role of a more senior, and perhaps, secured creditor (i.e., lender) and are generally more comfortable with established businesses, as opposed to start-up and early stage ventures. Venture capitalists, on the other hand, are typically more early stage investors, often in the form of equity (as opposed to debt), and are more willing to tolerate risk, particularly when they can identify strategies to help mitigate it. Given the difference in approach, individuals with venture capital experience can view an opportunity quite differently than a person with a banking background.

One of the main areas of interest is the "price" of the transaction, in terms of how much the business would have to pay (i.e., in terms of an acquisition) or how much the business would receive (i.e., in terms of a sale of the business) should a transaction occur. There is no one simple answer in terms of price, either. Details of the disposition can include cash payment, but also a range of other forms of remuneration (i.e., shareholdings, earn-outs, non-compete payments, directorships, consulting agreements, etc.).

The final amount is primarily based on the "range of value" of the business, as determined by a qualified business valuator, as well as the negotiations between the parties (i.e., based on the amount that one party is willing to pay and the amount that the other party is willing to accept).

There are various approaches to estimating value, most of which are quite technical in nature, but generally, may include looking at benchmarks for estimating value based on the nature of the business and/or industry, comparing to public company values, or similar transactions. The high degree of technicality in this area, as well as the need to apply judgment in terms of how valuation components should be used raises the importance of working with a qualified valuation advisor, such as a Chartered Business Valuator (CBV).

In the end, negotiated values can vary from the "technical" range of value determined by the business valuator. A strong desire to acquire the business (i.e., strategic value) or a strong motivation to sell the business (i.e., liquidation value) may affect the final value.

All of these issues should be considered by the family business leader and other shareholders in the business, in conjunction with qualified professional advisors, well in advance of a disposition, to avoid unfamiliarity with these concepts, but also to ready the business for its "best value" when the time comes. You want to be in the best prepared position when determining the various transaction options that the business could pursue.

Cultural Aspects of the Transaction

Once a family business undergoes a merger or takes on a significant partner it may no longer be the "family" business that it once was. In the case of an acquisition, this may not be the case; however, in the case of a sale of all or a substantial portion of the business, the "family" aspect of the business may cease to exist. The impact on the culture of the business when new parties come in or take over is something that should be carefully considered by the family business leader, as it may forever change the basis of the operation of the business.

In the case of an acquisition, this is expected, as new owners may choose to operate the business in a different manner than the family business leader, which may or may not be consistent with the values, beliefs, and practices of the previous ownership. In the case of a merger or bringing on of a significant partner, the impact on the culture of the business can be more problematic given that the family business leader (or members of the founding family) are typically still involved in the business on a day-to-day basis.

Situations may arise where the two parties are in conflict, perhaps over significant issues, in terms of how the business should be run, who should hold key roles in the business, which paths to growth should the business take, ethical issues, etc. The result can be a situation where the parties essentially cannot work together, resulting in damage to the business and perhaps another transaction to "reverse" the arrangement.

When a family business leader is considering the future of the business, in terms of growth-oriented transactions, succession to another party, or sale of the business, both the technical and cultural aspects of the options should be fully investigated, given the substantial impact that these transactions could have on the business going forward.

However, to begin, the business leader needs to ask him/herself: Is my most compelling role to continue to lead the operations of this business, or to steward the family's wealth and values to the next generation? The answer to this question can have a huge impact on both the family dynamics and that of the business, to propel its presence in the community from a leading commercial success to a significant and lasting legacy. To Master Your Investment in the Family Business, it's important to know when and how to do that.

THE SOLUTIONS

For various reasons already discussed, a succession plan is an integral part of the strategy of any business, and has a particular significance to family businesses. The family business leader must consider and plan for his or her exit at some point, in conjunction with various growth-oriented transactions along the way. This chapter will address some of these types of transactions.

Taking on a Partner

As in Paul's situation, one way in which a business can grow is to take on a partner who will bring their customer base or "book of business" to the company. This type of approach is more applicable to some industries, such as professional services (i.e., accountants, lawyers, etc.) or other types of service providers.

In this situation, one or more individuals may join the business, typically at a senior level, to create a larger customer and revenue base, thereby making the business larger. There are certainly benefits to this type of approach to growth, including relative ease of the transaction, ability to stage growth without taking on too much change at once, and ability of the family business leader to maintain control of the business, assuming that the new partner's book of business makes up less than half of the entire company after the transaction.

In this type of transaction, there is typically less of an impact on the culture of the business, as only one or a small number of individuals are being added to an existing and often larger business, which means that the new entrants are more likely to have to adapt to the existing culture, as opposed to bringing a new attitude and approach to doing things and imposing it on the business. There is also often an element of comfort, as the parties both work and have experience in the same industry or line of business, and as a team may be able to broaden their product or service offering to the benefit of the business and their customer base.

The partnership approach, however, is not without important selection criteria that should be fully addressed before undergoing this type of transaction, including the following:

- **Starting with non-disclosure, non-competition agreements.** There is nothing worse than walking down a path with a potential new partner only to find that the arrangement is not going to work. Any business partnership agreement must include a non-disclosure, non-compete clause. You certainly do not want to be exposing your business know-how to your next competitor. Further, you don't want your key employees to be enticed to leave. These issues must be identified and addressed up front in any new relationship.

- **The importance of partner selection.** The key to successfully undergoing this type of strategy is to choose potential partners very carefully and undergo a thorough due diligence and vetting process to ensure that the business opportunity is substantiated and that the potential partner has a work style and character that is consistent with the manner in which the family business operates. A qualified business advisor can be of assistance, possessing the necessary skills to conduct due diligence activities and the ability to provide an objective viewpoint. This is very important, as too many partnerships are not successful because the parties did not take the time to determine if they could work together. (The same can be said of some marriages, too!). The health of the business entity must always take precedence in the decision-making process. A qualified business advisor can project forward the potential of the enterprise, properly managed, and benefiting from the unique and complementary contributions of the partners.

- **The importance of implementation.** Agreeing which path to take and how implementation should occur can be a sensitive area, often resulting in differing opinions and dispute. Any partnership opportunity should have a plan, detailing how the transaction will occur and what changes will be necessary in both the new partner's current way of doing business, as well as in the existing family business. This approach will provide a clear path for implementation and address any areas of conflict before the transaction occurs, allowing the parties to determine if the transaction can successfully occur. There should also be a clear plan in terms of what happens when things don't go as planned—at the outset, and on an ongoing basis.

- **The importance of leverage.** An important component in terms of growing revenue and profitability is to carefully manage expenses, in that new partners should run most or their entire portion of the business utilizing existing staff members and resources within the family business, as opposed to bringing in their own cost structure (i.e., staff members, systems, etc.) and duplicating costs and effort. Leveraging off existing resources may be the initial strategy, but it is not uncommon for businesses that undergo this type of transaction to fail to take the necessary steps to implement the strategy, as it often involves specialized skills to do so and elimination of redundant positions.

Merging with Another Business

Merging your family business with another business has some similarities to the partnership model. However, a merger typically represents a more significant change to a business, as it may involve parties of a similar size and the dominant culture, leader, and approach going forward could be up for negotiation.

Two businesses of similar size may see benefits in coming together to broaden their product and service offering, increase the revenue and customer base of the business, and provide increased resources as a basis for achieving additional growth going forward.

There are many forms that a merger could take, all of which cannot be addressed here, but consider the following possible situations, which represent both opportunities and risks to the family business leader:

- **An opportunity for short-term growth** exists in the case where two parties can achieve growth together more rapidly than either party could alone. A merger transaction alone represents a larger business, and if managed properly, a more profitable business. Growth can occur more quickly than if the family business continued to operate on its own and grow through the normal course of acquiring customers. This type of situation can set up an opportunity five years into the future where the merged business may be large enough to attract the interest of a larger business, resulting in an acquisition that could provide an exit for the family business leader.

- **An opportunity for succession.** A family business leader may opt for a merger transaction in the absence of a succession plan, as the company that merges with the family business may have the succession resources to take the combined business forward at some future point in time.

- **Cultural risks.** As discussed in the partnership section, selecting a party to join forces with should be done very carefully, and this is of heightened importance under a merger scenario, due to the size and strength of the parties typically being more equal. If the family business leader does not select a party with a consistent approach and philosophy as to how the business should be operated, significant conflict and dispute could occur, which could damage the position of the business. Under a merger scenario, the family business leader may no longer be able to control how the business operates, which could put at risk their desire to be involved with the business going forward, as well as that of family members. This type of situation cannot continue to exist and may result in the business suffering, breaking apart, or ultimately being sold to one of the parties (or a third party), all of which can be costly and emotionally draining.

Mergers can represent complex transactions, and competent professional advice is required to provide the appropriate terms and conditions of the transaction and address due diligence and financing issues. The importance of selecting the "right" firm to merge with cannot be overstated, as the business could be fundamentally changed going forward. Once again, careful due diligence to confirm the strength of the company's products and services, management team, customer base, key systems, financial position, and character are of vital importance in terms of selecting an appropriate merger candidate.

Acquiring Another Business

A family business can approach growth by acquiring another business to create a larger revenue, customer, and perhaps resource basis with which to go forward. The difference between a merger and an acquisition is that, in the case of an acquisition, the family business will *retain its control* over the existing business, as well as the acquired business. In a merger transaction, control of the new entity is typically shared in some manner. This renders cultural issues of a lesser importance in the event of an acquisition, as the culture and approach of the acquiring company typically prevail.

However, what is of significant importance is verifying the substance of the opportunity, so that the actual opportunity is consistent with *what the family leader believes it to be.* This can be as straightforward as performing thorough due diligence to confirm the strength of the products and services, financial position, market potential, and management of the business, something that can be properly conducted with the assistance of a qualified business advisor or lawyer who knows how to conduct due diligence and what questions to ask. A greater challenge can be getting a sense of the character of the business, in terms of the manner in which the business operates, and assessing if this is an opportunity that is conducive to a successful acquisition. Although the acquirer ultimately will determine how the acquired business will operate, it is much easier to do so if the transition is smooth and a "battle" is not required.

An important component of this potentially problematic issue is to understand the role of existing staff members and their importance to the business, so that a plan can be developed to integrate and maintain these resources into the new structure going forward, or eliminate any resources that represent duplication or are not required. In the absence of a succession plan, the company being acquired may have resources that could succeed the family business leader at some point in the future, which can be a real benefit to the family business.

As with a merger, qualified professional advice is required to undergo this type of transaction. Specifically, how can this help? It takes a long time to know what drives a business forward, what made it successful in the past, and what will make it successful in the future. New owners often dismally fail at maximizing that potential because they quickly fall back to "doing it their way"; that is, instead of seeing the business and its independent potential, they think it's all about them. Professional advisors, properly utilized, can bring skills to develop new business plans suitable for new growth in what essentially is a new enterprise.

Sale of the Business

A sale transaction represents the most significant change to a family business, because, if the sale is made to an independent party, the business will no longer be a family business. This has important implications for both the family business leader and family members.

Family Business Leader

In the event of a sale transaction, the family business leader may no longer be a part of the business. This may be desired, or it may be a difficult transition. The family business leader has spent many years building the business and may have a strong attachment to it, as well as strong views as to how the business should be managed. With a new owner, these views may not be appreciated or of any relevance. And in fact, the new owner may not have the skills to take the business to its next stage of growth.

Opportunities may exist for the family business leader to continue to be involved with the business after the sale transaction, by way of contract or specified role where the founder can add value (i.e., technical areas, product development, customer relations, special projects, etc.). The new owner may benefit from having the family business leader remain with the business for a period of time to transition responsibilities or provide advice in certain areas.

This type of arrangement can be successful, as the family business leader typically has areas of expertise to pass to the new owners that could be helpful, but there can also be challenges. It may be difficult for a family business leader to be part of a business that they no longer control and they may not agree with some of the decisions and approaches being taken by the new owner. Since the family business leader is no longer in control, they typically will not have a role in decision making, which can lead to frustration and conflict. Family business leaders should be careful when considering this type of arrangement, and recognize that it may be difficult to fulfill.

What types of approaches can be taken to raise the likelihood of a successful transition? Here are a few to consider:

- **Short term contracts** of a year or less to help transition the business to the new owner can be workable, provided that the role is not a day-to-day management role in the business that includes decision-making power. This type of situation can be confusing and frustrating for staff members and the former business leader, as well as the new owner. The new owner must take the business forward, and be able to do so without interference, perceived or otherwise, from the former business leader. The idea here is for the former business leader to be a resource to help the new owner become familiar with the business and nothing more.

- **Working on a contract basis** in specific project areas can be helpful to both the former business leader and the new owner. This allows the former business leader to work on projects that may be of interest to them, perhaps utilizing their network to bring additional growth opportunities to the business. It may also allow the former owner to be compensated on a "success" basis, which means that the business only pays if the deal is closed.

- **Advisory arrangements**, for a specified period of time, where the former business leader is available to provide advice to the new owner outside of the day-to-day business operations can also be workable.

Should the family business leader wish to continue working in some capacity after the transaction, but not with the family business, careful consideration should be given to the impact and negotiation of non-compete clauses that may be part of the transaction. It is not uncommon for an acquirer to want to prohibit the family business member from starting a competing business or working with a competitor for a certain period of time after the sale transaction closes. Family business leaders should work closely with their advisors to understand the impact of such a requirement and negotiate accordingly, particularly in instances where the family business leader requires an income after the sale transaction is complete.

Entrepreneurs rarely retire—it's just not in their nature. Therefore, part of any sales transaction must include a clear glimpse into the "after-life" to properly manage expectations.

Family Members

In the case of family members who have a passive involvement in the business, a sale transaction may represent a sale of their shares (usually a good thing!) and the fact that the business no longer is a part of their lives. This can be a good thing, but it can also change family dynamics. The impact on family members who are actively involved in the business will be more significant, as they may also no longer have a job.

In the case of family members who continue to stay employed with the business after it is sold, they may be comfortable continuing under new ownership, but may be more likely to find it difficult to remain in this type of situation. They may not be comfortable with how the business is being managed or the direction that the business is moving, or may simply miss the way things used to be when the business was owned and managed by their family. This can result in family members choosing to leave the business and having to find alternate employment, which makes the terms and negotiation of any non-compete clause that is part of the sale transaction particularly important.

All family members will have to consider how they will replace the income that they were receiving from the family business, either actively or passively, and this is something that should be fully considered prior to the sale of the business. Qualified professional advisors can assist in structuring the sale transaction so that proceeds from the sale can be received in a manner that is tax effective for the recipients. However, the amount that is ultimately received is dependent upon the value of the business and the negotiations between the parties.

In short, a new "life plan" is required—for the business owner, the family members who worked in the business and other passive investors or interested parties, including employees, all of whom must cope with personal and financial change. This is stressful for most people. Add to this the fact that significant sums of money are often involved and you have a potential for a "perfect storm" through which skillful navigation and thoughtful preparedness are of considerable value.

Therefore, it goes without saying that a sale transaction is complex, and requires various qualified professional advisors to properly investigate, structure, and close. Receiving this type of qualified help can result in your investment in the family business being fully realized. Without it, many highly successful firms have met an early demise, to the great loss of the family, its employees, customers, and the community at large.

IN SUMMARY

Businesses can grow by their own efforts, by engaging partners, under-taking mergers or acquisitions, or embarking on an outright sale that may include ongoing participation by some family members. When this happens, both the family business leader and family members can be significantly affected and need to carefully consider how transactions of this nature could impact them and their lives.

Business transitions can create the opportunity for more significant growth, as opposed to growth achieved in the normal course of business, as well as represent succession opportunities for businesses that do not have a succession plan. Both the technical and cultural aspects of the transaction should be carefully considered, to ensure that the actual opportunity is consistent with what it appears to be and that the basis exists for the parties to be compatible. In circumstances where the family business leader or family members require an income after a sale transac-tion, careful consideration should be given to the structure and negotia-tion of non-compete clauses and ongoing involvement with the business.

Tax considerations cannot be underestimated, as a lifetime of work in building a family business can be swiftly eroded without the right tax structure for flowing proceeds of the sale.

Because these transactions are complex and specialized, qualified professional advice should be obtained.

THINGS YOU NEED TO KNOW

- There are various growth strategies that a business can take—through the course of normal operations (i.e., customer by customer), taking on a partner, merging the business, or acquiring a business.

- Business transactions can represent opportunities for succession and can be of particular use for a family business leader who does not have a succession plan. Examples include increased resources through a partnership, merger, or acquisition, or the family business leader selling their portion of the business to a partner or shareholders of a merged company at some future point in time.

- Bringing new partners into the business or merging the business can have an impact on the culture of the family business. New entrants may have approaches to doing things or a philosophy for running the business that is not consistent with that of the family business leader. That can "upset the apple cart", causing personal and financial implications.

- Business transactions are complex and require qualified professional advice in a number of areas to successfully occur.

QUESTIONS YOU NEED TO ASK

- Has there been a change in your succession plan that requires you to consider other options?

- Are there individuals or partners that are worthy of consideration as potential partners or candidates for a merger?

- Are there companies that should be investigated for potential acquisition?

- Do you have professional advisory resources that can assist you in conducting a business transaction?

- Are there reasons why the business should remain in the family or why it should be sold?

- In the event of a sale transaction, what are the income and ongoing employment requirements of family members?

THINGS YOU NEED TO DO

- Review your business plan and compare recent financial performance to determine if growth targets are being met. If actual performance is below what was budgeted or required, consider the impact of other options for growth, including partner, merger, and acquisition models.

- Review the competitive landscape of your industry and assess your performance and position. If your business is either in danger of falling behind or has been displaced in the market, consider options for growth.

- Consider what "life after the business" looks like and plan for that.

DECISIONS YOU NEED TO MAKE

- Determine your level of interest in terms of continuing to lead and grow the business. Consider the options for the business going forward and determine those that you believe to be worthy of investigation.

- Determine if the "business leaving the family" is a realistic option or not.

- Consider how to select the right advisors to help with the transition, merger, acquisition or sale.

MASTER YOUR INVESTMENT IN THE FAMILY BUSINESS
When the Business Leaves the Family

TIPS

- Carefully consider the impact of a business transaction on your company, particularly in terms of cultural fit and approach to doing business. Partners or merged companies that cannot work together can irreparably damage the business and be costly to unwind.

- Thoroughly investigate potential partner and merger candidates and take the time to get to know them.

- Decide whether these potential people are the right stewards of the future of the business, without you in it. If you want the business to survive independently of your guidance and control, this is your primary responsibility as its leader.

- Always get qualified professional advice when undergoing a business transaction. Those with a good level of experience in these transactions can usually work efficiently and provide much better advice than advisors with limited experience who may cost less.

TRAPS

- Continued involvement with a family business after a sale transaction should be considered carefully. The business may undergo considerable change, making it impossible for family members to be successfully integrated into the business.

- Carefully consider income requirements for family members going forward. Non-compete clauses may be structured in such a way that continued involvement in the industry for a period of time may not be permitted, which can lead to financial strain for family members. This is an area that must be carefully negotiated and understood.

Principle Mastery: Building a family business to a point where it has options for growth and succession, including by way of the normal course of operations, admitting partners, and making acquisitions provides strength in numbers for the business and the family. Choices, as opposed to forced options, are a good thing. This requires advance planning—it's never too early to start—as the right successor could be right around the corner.

CHAPTER 12

Moving Forward:
Stewardship and Philanthropy

The greatest use of a life is to spend it on something that will outlast it.
WILLIAM JAMES

Kim and Li Pak are a fairy tale "rags to riches" story. They left their native country many years ago and came to Canada with nothing more than a suitcase and hopes for a better life! Over the years, through sheer hard work, frugality and determination—and some good luck, they built up a network of retail stores across the country, selling high-end computer and wireless communications equipment. Today, they are on the verge of closing a deal to sell their stores to a large multi-national giant in the industry for over $50 million dollars.

Kim and Li Pak have always seemed to do the right thing. They have good financial, accounting, and tax advisors, and their business affairs are properly structured. While they've accomplished everything they hoped and dreamed for, there's something else they both feel they ought to do. While they obviously want to ensure that their kids and grandkids get a piece of their success, they also want people to know they made a difference! What should they do with all that money?

Kim suggested to Li Pak that they speak with their financial advisor on the matter. After all, they had counted on her advice over the years and had built a trusting professional relationship with their advisor.

THE ISSUES

Kim and Li Pak's financial advisor, Michelle Lemieux, congratulated them often on their outstanding accomplishments. To some degree, she felt pride in being a small part of their tremendous success along the way, as she listened to their thoughts on what they wanted to do with their incredible fortune.

Her clients had a number of things on their minds. They didn't want to waste their good fortune and they certainly wanted to benefit not only their children and grandchildren but also create a lasting mark or legacy that would continue to benefit their community. They understood that their business had an important economic impact for many families.

Kim was also concerned about the amount of taxes they would have to pay on the sale and wondered what could be done about that.

Both were clear that they liked to maintain control over their money and how it might be used to benefit their community.

After a lengthy discussion, Michelle summarized the key issues for Kim and Li Pak as follows:

- How to minimize taxes on the sale of the company
- How to provide for family wealth transition
- How to create a lasting legacy

Minimizing taxes on the sale of the company. This couple, together with their advisors over the years, had done a great job of structuring and positioning their companies to minimize taxes. While their kids and grandkids were not actively involved in the business, they would be able to access the $750,000 Lifetime Capital Gains Exemption through the use of an *inter vivos* family trust. However, even with this good planning, the overall tax bite would be significant on a 50 million dollar sale. Their financial advisor suggested that they might consider making a significant gift to charity in the year of sale, in order to offset a bigger chunk of the capital gains tax otherwise payable.

Providing for family wealth transition. Also identified was the need to re-visit their wills and overall estate plan. Their financial advisor suggested that there were strategies that they could implement to tax-efficiently transition wealth to their children and grandchildren, including the use of testamentary and "springing" trusts. These are areas that should be reviewed with their lawyer and tax advisor in some detail, the advisor recommended.

Creating a lasting legacy. Perhaps one of the most significant opportunities for Kim and Li Pak was their ability to create something to benefit their community on a lasting basis. Their financial advisor pointed out that there were a number of different "vehicles" and strategies by which they could make a significant charitable gift, including an outright donation to a charity, a gift to a "donor-advised" fund, a charitable remainder trust, or perhaps a private charitable foundation.

Kim and Li Pak took a moment to refill their coffee cups and then sat down as their financial advisor continued to explain their options.

THE SOLUTIONS

Kim and Li Pak were particularly interested in the last two issues identified by their financial advisor. Obviously, they intended to leave a good chunk of their wealth to their children and grandchildren, but they wanted to hear more about their options in terms of charitable giving. Also, if they could save some tax now, that would even be better!

"We also want to have a say on how our money is used," Li Pak stressed. This is a sentiment many affluent families have on their minds today.

Michelle outlined a number of things that Kim and Li Pak should consider in terms of their plans to transition the family's wealth.

Providing for Family Wealth Transition

"First," she said, "you should know that most of the proceeds received on the sale of your companies will be realized within the *inter vivos* trust. While you and all of the family members will each take advantage of the $750,000 Lifetime Capital Gains Deduction, a significant portion of the gain will still be subject to tax.

"The trustees have the discretionary power to either pay out the capital to one or more beneficiaries or retain the funds within the trust. Since the *inter vivos* trust already constitutes an excellent means of transitioning your wealth, the trustees could choose to retain the capital within the trust and undertake a stewardship role to grow and manage the family wealth.

"Depending on the jurisdiction in which a trust is resident, provincial or territorial trust law will generally provide for a rule against perpetuities and accumulations. This means that the trust cannot continue indefinitely or into perpetuity. However, Manitoba alone, amongst the various provinces and territories, has abolished the rule against perpetuities and accumulations in its entirety. This would permit an *inter vivos* trust with a Manitoba tax residence to continue into perpetuity for your grandchildren and great-grandchildren. Such trusts are typically described as 'dynasty trusts', since they can virtually last forever.

"Since your trust is resident in Manitoba," continued Michelle, "you may wish to consider using the *inter vivos* trust as the receptacle to steward your family wealth. However, be aware that even though the trust can continue for many generations to come, there are tax rules that will require the *inter vivos* trust to recognize a deemed realization of its assets (and potentially pay tax on any resulting capital gains) every 21 years from its inception. Even so, this can be an excellent way to manage, preserve and grow the family wealth. You may also consider engaging institutional trustees to do so," she added. "That way, there is built-in continuity to ensure that the family wealth is professionally managed, regardless of the ability or lack of ability of your future heirs and successors."

Further, on Kim or Li Pak's death, assets vested within the trust would not fall within their estate, nor would such assets be subject to the provisions contained within their will. The *inter vivos* trust would continue as a free-standing receptacle, with the family wealth therein remaining intact and subject only to the provisions contained within the trust document.

"Of course," Michelle continued, "another option is to pay out a significant portion of the capital of the trust to yourselves during your lifetime."

The trust was initially settled by Kim's father, with both Kim and Li Pak identified as potential capital beneficiaries in the original trust document.

To the extent that Kim and Li Pak do receive trust capital, such assets will form part of their estate for testamentary purposes, and therefore any succession plan would be subject to the terms of their will.

"Where this is the case," Michelle noted, "your wills can provide for the creation of separate testamentary trusts for your children and grandchildren. In effect, your estate residue could fund each testamentary trust and you could, if you so desired, create a separate testamentary trust for each individual beneficiary."

"Why would we want to do that?" Li Pak inquired.

"Well, each testamentary trust is subject to tax as a separate individual person under the Income Tax Act, and each such trust would then enjoy the benefits of having its income taxed at lower progressive tax rates in the same manner as an individual taxpayer. Doing so enables you to create multiple testamentary trusts and thereby achieve substantial tax savings by income splitting with each testamentary trust," their financial advisor explained.

"Of course, the family wealth gets somewhat fragmented if it is divided up between your children, grandchildren, or even great-grandchildren. Management and stewardship of the family wealth would likely also no longer be maintained under common control. This could become a concern in certain circumstances, particularly if there are issues about passing wealth directly to your children or grandchildren, or pressure from outside parties, including creditors or from the personal relationships of your heirs.

"You might also structure certain 'springing' trusts, so called because they come into existence only upon the death of the primary beneficiary. For instance, your will might provide for the creation of a testamentary trust for each child, and then separate testamentary trusts to receive the trust residue either on the death of that child or on a last-to-die with your child's spouse or common-law partner.

"There are a substantial number of possibilities in structuring your overall estate and wealth succession plan," concluded Michelle. "You should consult with an estate and trust lawyer and your tax accountant to outline a plan tailored to your own situation."

"Hmmm, sounds good to me," said Kim. "What about using a holding company?"

"Yes, that is another possibility," Michelle agreed. "You could personally transfer some of your wealth realized on the sale to a newly incorporated holding company. In so doing, you could also implement an estate freeze in favour of the *inter vivos* trust, or in favour of your intended successors directly. There are advantages and disadvantages in using this structure. Unlike an *inter vivos* trust, there is no deemed realization of assets within a corporation every 21 years. Therefore, the opportunity exists to maintain, grow and steward the family wealth effectively within the corporate vehicle."

However, Michelle cautioned them about some disadvantages of direct ownership in the holding company shares by children or grandchildren. These can include:

- Potential claims by the children's creditors;
- Marital property claims; and
- Capital gains taxes arising on the death of a family shareholder.

"Of course, one of the advantages of using a holding company structure is that the shares can be easier to transfer or deal with, as opposed to specific investment assets," observed the financial advisor.

"Once again, I strongly recommend that you review this aspect of your wealth succession plan with your tax accountant and legal advisor. I would be happy to help set up a joint meeting so that all of us can meet together to review your options," she concluded. "Why don't we now discuss some of the aspects pertaining to your charitable giving plans?"

Creating a Lasting Legacy

The advisor explained the basic "nuts and bolts" of how a number of charitable giving options worked.

An Outright Donation to Charity

An outright donation to a charity is the most direct and straightforward way to make a gift and get immediate tax relief.

"The advantage of doing this in the year you sell your business is that the donation tax credit (worth roughly 46 cents on the dollar) can be used to offset capital gains taxes," Michelle noted. "Since the maximum capital gains tax rate is approximately 23 per cent, every dollar donated to charity will cover two dollars of capital gains. Not only that," she continued, "recent federal budget changes have eliminated the capital gains tax payable when a charitable donation of publicly-traded securities, including shares, bonds and mutual funds, is made.

"This is a very effective way to make a substantial gift within the community, while reducing your taxes in the year of sale," she added. "You might consider gifting some of your existing stock portfolio and retain the cash you get on the sale of your business."

"But how much say will we have with the charity over how they spend our money?" asked Kim.

"Well, with a simple gift to charity, the gift must be irrevocable and you effectively lose control over how the capital is disbursed," was the answer.

"That's not so good," said Li Pak. "We intend to make a sizable donation of at least three to five million dollars, and we would like to have some control over how the money is used."

"Yes," added Kim. "We were thinking that we could direct funds toward our community—perhaps for a new cultural centre, or to support our heritage and education of young people."

"Those are great ideas," their financial advisor noted, before going on to explain other more complex arrangements for such charitable giving.

Charitable Remainder Trust

A gift to a charity through a charitable remainder trust (CRT) is becoming more frequently used. Kim and Li Pak listened carefully as they learned about this option. In effect, they could set up a trust today, contribute the property to the trust, but provide under the terms of trust that the property vest with the charity at some later date.

"You might for instance, contribute $3 million today to a CRT, but provide that the funds only transfer to the charity upon the last to die or perhaps within a defined period of time," explained the advisor.

"Why would we do that?" asked Li Pak.

"Well, you might wish to continue to earn and enjoy the income from the trust during your lifetime, but provide that the charity receives the funds upon the last death. If you do that, the value of your gift today for tax purposes would be the net present value of the amount gifted, actuarially determined, based on your life expectancies. A CRT is a way to make a gift today, get a tax receipt for doing so, and defer the transfer to charity to some later date."

"Could we make the gift through our will?" asked Kim.

"Yes, but the donation tax credit would not be available until the gift is made and then the donation tax credit can only be claimed on the date of death return or carried back and used in the tax year immediately preceding the terminal return. Depending on the income reported on the terminal return and the size of the bequest, your executors might not be able to fully utilize the entire donation. It would be a pity to waste the tax benefits associated with such a large gift," said Michelle. "As I mentioned earlier, the real advantage lies in using the donation tax credit today to offset your capital gains taxes.

"A CRT set up during your lifetime today would accomplish just that. Control over capital can be maintained. The only drawback is that the gift to charity is deferred, so that your donation dollars will not be serving the community needs until the property vests with the charity. For all these reasons, CRTs are generally used to provide a continuing income to a beneficiary and then a transfer to charity on the death of that beneficiary."

"Hmm," Li Pak frowned. "No, we would like to do something right away. We want to see that we are making a difference."

"Okay," Michelle acknowledged. "Let's look at another gifting alternative."

Donor-Advised Funds

A number of financial institutions now offer programs featuring donor designated and donor-advised charitable funds. The main features that distinguish this type of program from that of an outright gift to charity are the following:

- A donor's charitable contribution is pooled with a separate account balance maintained for each donor. In some cases, the financial institution maintains the investment in a segregated fund to specifically identify the capital each donor contributed.

- A donor has the right to recommend qualified tax-exempt organizations to receive distributions from the fund. In effect, each donor can direct these funds to the charities and causes that mean the most to them. If the donor's recommendation is not accepted by the fund trustee, the trustee will make an alternate distribution.

- Contributions to the fund should qualify for a current donation tax credit.

- The fund creates a separate sub-account for each donor, but the trustees maintain ownership of the sub-account assets; the donor can exercise only the rights set out in the trust document.

- Each donor can also involve his or her family in the decision-making process for grants each year and can name a family member to succeed them as advisor for such grants from the donor-advised funds after the donor's death.

The couple's financial advisor explained that a donor's sub-account is subject to certain fund fees charged for the administration, accounting and management of the donor-advised pooled funds.

"The advantage of this type of planned giving is that you do not need to incur any up-front costs to set up the fund, nor do you need to deal with the ongoing administration, legal and accounting for the fund. Plus, you are entitled to the tax savings up-front as soon as you make the contribution. That can be quite useful in reducing your overall capital gains tax burden today, while providing you with the future flexibility to exercise some level of control over how the funds are disbursed. And, you get to see and feel good about how your donation is being used today and throughout your lifetime!"

"Wow! That sounds a lot more like what we want to do," said Kim. "But, I also heard something about private foundations. Doesn't that option give us the best of everything?"

That certainly was another option for this couple, as Michelle outlined next.

Private Charitable Foundation

A private charitable foundation will usually be created as a company with no issued share capital. Its Board of Directors can consist of family members who then can collectively exercise control over the assets of the foundation and make decisions about disbursements or gifts to qualified donees.

There are a lot of advantages in using a private foundation, according to the financial advisor, including:

- An immediate tax receipt for a donation made to the foundation;
- Control over where and to whom the foundation disburses funds;
- The creation of a "legacy" and ongoing recognition within the community; and
- The opportunity to involve children and grandchildren (as directors) in the good work the foundation can do in the community.

For some, a private charitable foundation works well, because it provides the cement to keep family members active and working together in the community in support of the legacy left to them.

However, there are also some pretty big disadvantages if you go down that route, Michelle cautioned. The main disadvantages include:

- Significant up-front costs to set up the foundation (legal and accounting);
- A requirement for formalized accounting and tax compliance reporting, which can add up to a substantial annual cost and time commitment;
- New tax reporting rules and restrictions where a private foundation holds shares in private unlisted companies, or more than two percent of listed publicly-traded securities;

- The requirement to be actively involved in the decision making to ensure that the private foundation meets its 80 percent disbursement quota requirement. Unlike involvement with a "donor-advised" fund, being a Board member on a private foundation is a much more time-consuming commitment.

The financial advisor concluded by suggesting that a private charitable foundation should ideally be considered where the gift is in the $5 to $10 million range.

"Otherwise," she said, "the annual costs of compliance and the ongoing work to administer the foundation will outweigh the benefits you can gain from going a simpler route."

Kim and Li Pak had a lot to think about. But their visit to their financial advisor had been fruitful, and they looked forward to making their decisions with the help of their lawyer and tax professional as well.

They were particularly interested in the lasting stewardship of their gift. They would need to broach the subject with their heirs and let them know more about their philosophy and directions for the preservation and orderly distribution of their incredible wealth.

IN SUMMARY

This chapter focused on the main issues relating to a founder's wealth succession and philanthropic intentions and the different ways that wealth can be stewarded, while structuring a significant and meaningful gift to charity.

Decisions pertaining to the wealth succession plan will depend on the structure used to maintain the family wealth, namely:

- Use of an *inter vivos* discretionary family trust;
- Personally held wealth governed by the testator's will; or
- Use of a holding company to act as the receptacle for family wealth.

Decisions around the timing and structure of the gift will depend on the following factors:

- The need for an immediate tax donation receipt;
- The level of direction the donor wishes to maintain over the donated funds; and
- The complexity and ongoing involvement the donor is willing to take on to structure the gift.

To be eligible for a donation tax credit, a gift must be made to a registered charity or foundation and the transfer must be irrevocable. Also, it is important to distinguish the difference between the terms "donor-advised" and "donor-directed". A donor-advised fund should meet CRA's test for an "irrevocable" gift, whereas a donor-directed fund could easily fail this test and therefore not constitute a bona-fide donation for tax purposes.

To be eligible for a donation tax credit, the donor can make recommendations to the fund trustee within the scope of the trust document. However, a donor cannot exercise complete control over the destination of the capital. If this were the case, then an irrevocable gift would not be considered to have been made, and the tax advantages of the donation could be lost.

Look for the title, *Master Your Philanthropy* by Nicola Elkins, in this
Master Your Personal Finances series. This book provides more detailed
information about a strategic plan for family giving activities.

THINGS YOU NEED TO KNOW

Stewardship
- Manitoba alone, amongst the provinces and territories in Canada,
  allows for the establishment of a dynasty trust, so that family
  wealth can be preserved and stewarded for many generations.
- The 21-year rule is relevant in terms of assets held by any *inter
  vivos* family trust.
- The corporate ownership structure is a vital component in creating
  an overall wealth succession plan. The tax considerations vary considerably depending on whether assets are held personally, in a
  corporation, or within a trust.
- Testamentary trusts can be used in a testator's will planning for a
  variety of estate, tax, and income splitting objectives.

Philanthropy
- A significant donation or gift is best made in the year in which
  you are reporting significant income, such as would be the case
  where the family business is sold.
- Every dollar of donation made covers the tax bill on two dollars of
  capital gains realized.
- Gifts can be made during your lifetime (*inter vivos*) or on death
  (*testamentary*) by virtue of the will. In the latter situation, the
  donation can be used in the year of death and the immediately
  preceding taxation year. Large bequests on death can be ineffective
  from a tax standpoint, unless there is enough income to soak up
  the donation tax credit.

- There are several ways to structure a tax-efficient gift to charity, including:
  - An outright donation;
  - The use of a charitable remainder trust;
  - Donor-advised funds; and
  - A private charitable foundation.
- Gifts of capital property, including publicly trades shares, bonds, and mutual funds get special tax treatment in that any resulting gain to the donor is tax-free.

QUESTIONS YOU NEED TO ASK

Stewardship

- What extent of control do we wish to exercise over our heirs and successors?
- What are the tax implications to the estate on a last-to-die scenario?
- What are the tax consequences pertaining to various structures, including personally-held wealth, corporations or trusts?
- What structure is best for our family?

Philanthropy

- When is the best time for me to make a charitable donation?
- What amount of donation will optimize my tax savings?
- What are the costs associated with using a slightly more complex structure, such as a charitable remainder trust or a donor-advised fund?
- Do I need to provide for continuing income to a beneficiary ahead of any charitable purpose?
- Are my children or grandchildren interested in the charitable giving process? How can I get them involved?

THINGS YOU NEED TO DO

Stewardship

- Review your will with a view to assessing how family wealth will be transitioned. Are your objectives met?
- Determine the tax impact to your estate on a last-to-die scenario.
- Evaluate the various structures (personal, corporate, trusts) to understand how each different structure impacts your wealth succession plans.

Philanthropy

- Review your tax affairs to determine optimal donation amounts for tax purposes.
- Review your plans with your advisors, who can explore and explain all of the gifting alternatives to you.
- Discuss your intentions with family, particularly when it comes to a substantial gift. Sometimes family members can misinterpret your intentions!

DECISIONS YOU NEED TO MAKE

Stewardship
- Make decisions as to how the family wealth will be transitioned and divided between heirs and successors, as well as charity.
- Determine the level of control you wish to impose over your heirs. Do they get the assets directly, or is it appropriate to defer ownership with the use of trusts?
- Decide on a structure to optimize your objectives, control and tax-efficiency.

Philanthropy
- Decide whether a long-term legacy gift is appropriate for you and your family.
- Determine an appropriate gift amount to optimize your tax savings.
- Decide whether control or direction over donated funds is critical to you and your family. This will assist you in determining your donation structure.
- Decide whether it is important to make a gift during your lifetime or whether you wish to do so through your will.

MASTER YOUR INVESTMENT IN THE FAMILY BUSINESS
Moving Forward: Stewardship and Philanthropy

TIPS

- Be as flexible as you can with the overall wealth succession plan. Put your trust in your executors, administrators, and trustees and give them broad powers to make the right decisions.
- Don't try to control too much on a post-mortem basis.
- Always consider the tax "implications" of making a gift. The donation credit is precious and can only be carried forward for five taxation years.
- Select a donation strategy and structure which suits your long-term objectives and commitment to the process. If you like things to be simple and uncomplicated, it is always best in the long run to go with a structure that affords this treatment.

TRAPS

- Be careful not to "over-complicate" your tax affairs in the course of structuring an estate and wealth succession plan or in your overall gift and legacy planning.
- If you involve family members as trustees or directors, be aware that differences of opinion may arise as to how the funds are administered. What may seem like a good idea to bring family members together to administer family wealth or perhaps to manage a common charitable cause might also divide them.

Principle Mastery: Use the appropriate wealth succession and donation strategies wisely, in keeping with family goals and commitment to involvement, in order to maximize the family's lasting wealth and legacy.

Conclusions

The investment you have in your business can easily represent the most significant portion of the family's overall wealth. Throughout this book, a number of fundamental concepts for managing and **Mastering Your Investment in the Family Business** have been highlighted. These are summarized below:

1. Seek qualified professional advisors that have the necessary skills and experience for the appropriate issue at hand. The cost of not doing so can be significant.

2. Dare to be a Market Driven Family Business; the marketplace needs qualified, customer-focused service and product providers. Why not let your business fill this need and also benefit financially?

3. Family businesses are much more than "just a family business". You should create and foster an environment to set performance goals for family and non-family members alike.

4. The corporate structure of the family business is the key to minimizing tax and optimizing cash flows to the business owners. Obtain professional tax advice to optimize the corporate structure.

5. Create a business plan to deal effectively with growth and personnel issues, and effectively manage crisis situations.

6. Recognize that cash flows and family wealth can be maximized by corporate financing, wherever possible.

7. Communicate your vision. Share your plans with family and key employees and be "inclusive". Remember that the sum of a whole is always greater than each separate part.

8. Challenge yourself, your family members, and your professional advisors to work strategically as a team, and include a focus on continuing education and professional development. Issues change, markets change, and in that change lies the key to success—if you can think, analyze and question well enough to anticipate it.

9. Plan for business succession and also look outside or beyond the family to ensure that the right individuals are part of the family business. Recognize that the life cycle of the family business and the family business leader need not be the same.

10. Create a lasting legacy through your business and philanthropic endeavors. Remember that "the greatest use of a life is to spend it on something that will outlast it." [WILLIAM JAMES].

Index

Other Titles in
The Knowledge Bureau's
Master Your Series